MACMILLAN MODERN DRAMATISTS

Macmillan Modern Dramatists

Series Editors: *Bruce King* and *Adele King*

Published titles

Reed Anderson, *Federico Garcia Lorca*
Eugene Benson, *J. M. Synge*
Renate Benson, *German Expressionist Drama*
Normand Berlin, *Eugene O'Neill*
Michael Billington, *Alan Ayckbourn*
Roger Boxill, *Tennessee Williams*
John Bull, *New British Political Dramatists*
Dennis Carroll, *David Mamet*
Neil Carson, *Arthur Miller*
Maurice Charney, *Joe Orton*
Ruby Cohn, *New American Dramatists, 1960–1980*
Bernard F. Dukore, *American Dramatists, 1918–1945*
Bernard F. Dukore, *Harold Pinter*
Arthur Ganz, *George Bernard Shaw*
James Gibbs, *Wole Soyinka*
Frances Gray, *John Arden*
Frances Gray, *Noel Coward*
Charles Hayter, *W. S. Gilbert and Arthur Sullivan*
Julian Hilton, *Georg Büchner*
David Hirst, *Edward Bond*
Helene Keyssar, *Feminist Theatre*
Bettina L. Knapp, *French Theatre 1918–1939*
Charles Lyons, *Samuel Beckett*
Gerry McCarthy, *Edward Albee*
Jan McDonald, *The New Drama 1900–1914*
Susan Bassnett-McGuire, *Luigi Pirandello*
Margery Morgan, *August Strindberg*
Leonard C. Pronko, *Eugene Labiche and Georges Feydeau*
Jeanette L. Savona, *Jean Genet*
Claude Schumacher, *Alfred Jarry and Guillaume Apollinaire*
Laurence Senelick, *Anton Chekhov*
Theodore Shank, *American Alternative Theatre*
James Simmons, *Sean O'Casey*
Ronald Speirs, *Bertolt Brecht*
David Thomas, *Henrik Ibsen*
Dennis Walder, *Athol Fugard*
Thomas Whitaker, *Tom Stoppard*
Nick Worrall, *Nikolai Gogol and Ivan Turgenev*
Katharine Worth, *Oscar Wilde*

MACMILLAN MODERN DRAMATISTS

DAVID MAMET

Dennis Carroll
Professor of Drama and Theatre
University of Hawaii at Manoa

MACMILLAN

First published 1987

Published by
Higher and Further Education Division
MACMILLAN PUBLISHERS LTD
Houndmills, Basingstoke, Hampshire RG21 2XS
and London
Companies and representatives
throughout the world

Typeset by Wessex Typesetters
(Division of The Eastern Press Ltd)
Frome, Somerset

Printed in Hong Kong

British Library Cataloguing in Publication Data
Carroll, Dennis
David Mamet.—(Modern dramatists)
1. Mamet, David—Criticism and
interpretation
I. Title   II. Series
812'.54   PS3563.A4345Z/
ISBN 0-333-41365-2
ISBN 0-333-41366-0 Pbk

Contents

To Elsa

List of Plates

Editors' Preface

The *Macmillan Modern Dramatists* is an international series of introductions to major and significant nineteenth- and twentieth-century dramatists, movements and new forms of drama in Europe, Great Britain, America and new nations such as Nigeria and Trinidad. Besides new studies of great and influential dramatists of the past, the series includes volumes on contemporary authors, recent trends in the theatre and on many dramatists, such as writers of farce, who have created theatre 'classics' while being neglected by literary criticism. The volumes in the series devoted to individual dramatists include a biography, a survey of the plays, and detailed analysis of the most significant plays, along with discussion, where relevant, of the political, social, historical and theatrical context. The authors of the volumes, who are involved with theatre as playwrights, directors, actors, teachers and critics, are concerned with the plays as theatre and discuss such matters as performance, character interpretation and staging, along with themes and contexts.

Bruce King
Adele King

Acknowledgements

Work on the present book was made exciting and enjoyable by several strangers who gave me prompt courtesy and co-operation while I was off home turf. I am grateful to them for information, guidance through unpublished material, copies of scripts and other matter, and helping with copyright permissions.

In Chicago, I should like to thank Sheila Ryan, Specialist for the Goodman and St Nicholas Theatre Archives, Special Collections, Chicago Public Library; and Jennifer Boznos, Press Director of the Goodman Theatre. In New York, Mr Howard Rosenstone and Mr John Gersten of Rosenstone/Wender; Mr Andrew Wylie; Mr Derek Johns of Random House; and Mr David Brown of the Zanuck/ Brown Company. Thanks also to Mrs Betty L. Corwin, Project Director of Theatre on Film and Tape (TOFT), Billy Rose Theatre Collection, New York Public Library at Lincoln Center, and her staff for arranging tape-viewings for me.

I should especially like to thank David Mamet, not only for granting me an interview, but also for his co-operation in letting me study unpublished material and work in progress.

In Honolulu, Bernard F. Dukore, my senior colleague, who is now University Distinguished Professor of Theatre Arts and Humanities at Virginia Tech, knew of my interest in Mamet's work and recommended me for this assignment; Ann Takahashi, Librarian at the University of Hawaii at Manoa, searched material promptly and established some valuable library contacts; and my son Eero read through the manuscript and made some good suggestions.

Quotations from David Mamet's plays have been taken from the American editions listed in the Bibliography. Videotapes of Mamet productions described are held in the TOFT Collection, Billy Rose Theatre Collection, New York Public Library at Lincoln Center, and are also listed in the Bibliography. Dates given after the plays' titles in the text are those not of writing or publication, but of first performance of the definitive version.

I would also like to thank the publishers Faber and Faber Ltd and Viking Penguin for permission to quote from Mamet's *Writing in Restaurants*.

1
Mid-Career

On 1 November 1975, *New York Times* critic Mel Gussow heralded the 'auspicious New York debut' of a new playwright.[1] David Mamet's *Sexual Perversity in Chicago* and *The Duck Variations* had opened in a showcase production at the St Clements Theatre off-off-Broadway. Meanwhile back in Chicago an even more important premiere had taken place. On 21 October, *American Buffalo* (1975) began its career at the Goodman Theatre Stage Two, broke all box-office records for the series, and transferred to Mamet's own St Nicholas Theatre as the inaugural offering in its new premises. Richard Christiansen, the Chicago critic, said later of the *American Buffalo* opening that 'if you're looking for significant dates in the history of Chicago – and American – theatre, there's one to remember'.[2]

Mamet's acclaim was not sudden or unanimous – it came in fits and starts. The Broadway opening of *American Buffalo* in 1977 did not meet with the critical rave notices accorded a *Death of a Salesman* or a *Who's Afraid of*

1

Virginia Woolf? In that same year, however, three other Mamet plays were unveiled in Chicago and New York – and *A Life in the Theatre*, especially, received fulsome reviews. Then in 1979, stung by some critical reverses, Mamet began a second career in screenwriting. At the same time he was far from idle in the theatre, though major plays came with longer intervals. Several of his early plays were restaged and reassessed; in 1983 *American Buffalo* reached Broadway for the second time and was now hailed as one of the most significant plays of the decade. By 1984 Mamet's awards included three Chicago Jefferson Awards for best new play of the season, two *Village Voice* Obies, two New York Drama Critics' Circle Awards, the English SWET (Society of West End Theatres) Award, the John Gassner Award, the Outer Critics' Circle Award for services to the American theatre, an Oscar nomination, and the Pulitzer Prize for *Glengarry Glen Ross* (1983). Though most critics were now in agreement that Mamet had arrived, they were not always sure how or where. No sooner was Mamet called a chronicler of shapeless low-life than he appeared to change direction and write in a sparer manner on a wider variety of subjects; no sooner did he seem to espouse more optimistic visions of human contact than he returned to the more cryptically equivocal attitudes of *Edmond* (1982) and *Glengarry Glen Ross*.

It is now apparent that Mamet is the only playwright of several who emerged as 'promising' in the late 1970s – including Christopher Durang, Albert Innaurato, Beth Henley and Michael Cristofer – who has so far managed to establish a significant international reputation. He has created a body of work which reveals complex variations rather than mere repetitive obsessiveness; synthesised American and European traditions of twentieth-century drama in a way that preserves an individual signature;

captured the interest of large audiences; created plays in which characters walk a fine line between despair and hope, dissolution and integration, solitude and communion. Dichotomies, paradoxes and dialectical tensions are central to his work, and apparent in the personality he projects.

Mamet has two different personae which register in the many interviews he has given. They have class overtones. Alan Gross, a fellow Chicago playwright, described him in 1978 as being an 'interesting combination of South Side tough guy and rich kid'.[3] He can give the impression of being a flinty, street-smart cynic distrustful of easily won communicativeness, the whole peppered with a wacky humour and reinforced by his stocky build, short hair and plain dress. But he also appears as well-read and intelligent on his own plays and aims, as a moralist who passionately believes in the theatre's power for communion, as a teacher who inveighs against the ersatz in life and in art. The tension between the two personae might well produce the air of combativeness which several interviewers have noted in the man. There is a tension between his actual words, seemingly chosen and edited with calculated precision, and the warmly involved air of spontaneity with which he delivers them. In his plays, a similar tension can exist between the words themselves and the intent and rhythms that drive them; many plays give evidence of a tough cynicism on the surface and a positive will to contact underlying it.

Dialectical tensions abound in Mamet's life and career. They include his family's Polish–Jewish background on the one hand, and a desire to assimilate with a larger sense of being American on the other; the need for blue-collar exuberance and informality as well as middle-class restraint and stability; the early humdrum world of Chicago high-school reality set against nascent alternative worlds of the imagination fired by his first contacts with theatre; the early uncertainty about whether to concentrate on performing or writing; the conflict about whether to remain as artistic director of his own regional theatre or to drive towards national recognition as a playwright; the attractions of screenwriting as against those of writing for the theatre; the pull of rural Vermont against the urban centres; the split in affiliation between Chicago and New York. There are also the dichotomies both within and between the plays themselves. There are Apollonian plays which present formal poise and positive human control in the ascendant, and Dionysian plays careening with the compulsions of characters desperate to create new worlds for themselves and sometimes destroying themselves and others in the process.

David Alen Mamet was born on 30 November 1947, and spent his early years in Flossmoor, a suburb of Chicago about twenty-six miles south of the central 'Loop' area.[4] His grandfather came of Polish–Jewish stock, his father was a labour lawyer, and his mother, also of Jewish background, was a schoolteacher. Mamet felt later that his parents had downplayed their own cultural heritage in order to assimilate – they were both children of immigrants. His father was an amateur semanticist who would often insist at dinner that Mamet and his sister Lyn find the exact words to best express themselves. Lyn later suggested in an interview that her brother probably saw the motive for this kind of training not as pure, but as expression of a conviction that 'life is horrible and you better be good at something. I don't think he felt loved for just being David'.[5] The training surely influenced Mamet's command of verbal precision; and his talent for the sound of words and their rhythm was further sharpened by piano lessons from 1951 and his study of complicated rhyming jingles on records put out by the International Society of Semanticists.

In 1957–8 his parents were divorced. For a time, Mamet lived with his mother and sister in the suburb of South Shore. Then the three moved to a 'model suburb' adjacent to Flossmoor called Olympia Fields, where they lived in a tiny home which epitomised middle-class repression to Mamet. He started high school at Rich Central High; as he thought he was a poor student, in spite of voracious reading, he began to develop alternative worlds for the drab life around him.

These were shaped first through sport, then through the theatre. At Rich, he broke his nose playing football, and took up wrestling. Theatre attracted him because of the energy that theatre people have and because they seemed to work so much on instinct. Theatre became even more important after he went to live in the near North (Lincoln Park) area of the city with his father in 1963, and transferred to the Francis Parker school, a prestigious private school founded in 1903. Parker had a well-developed drama programme, and Mamet took courses and played the lead in a musical. The school was close to several community and professional theatres which enlivened Chicago theatrical life in the 1960s.

From 1963 to 1965, Mamet worked both at Hull House and at Second City, the famed improvisational comedy troupe that had been founded in 1959. He got practical theatrical experience at Hull House, which, under Bob Sickinger's direction, did many forthright and intense productions from an adventurous repertory at the Jane Addams auditorium. Mamet worked backstage in Schisgal's *The Typists* and *The Tiger*; he was in the chorus of Brecht's *The Threepenny Opera* and played a stretcher-bearer in Kenneth Brown's *The Brig*. At Second City he worked as a 'general dogsbody' front of house, but the revue-like structure of the Second City evenings, the short scenes separated by blackouts, were an influence on his early work.

After he had left high school, Mamet's father wanted him to study law; instead, Mamet enrolled at Goddard College in Vermont. For the first time he lived in a rural environment: the college was situated at Plainfield, ten miles east of Montpelier on hilly farmland. The resident student body was small, and the college itself exemplified educational liberalism. There were no required courses, no grades and no examinations. Mamet was enrolled for a BA in English literature; and there was a 'junior year abroad' concept, in which two semesters had to be spent in non-resident workstudy.

Mamet's 'junior year abroad' in New York City had effects on him which were to be profound and long-lasting. He decided to spend his time – in 1967–8 – studying acting at the Neighborhood Playhouse, where the famed Group Theatre alumnus Sanford Meisner and his staff taught a Stanislavsky-derived system of acting adapted from what was known of the Method of Physical Actions. Mamet took only the first year of what was a two-year course. It influenced his later work as director and acting-teacher and his writing and script-analysis techniques. Emphasis was placed on intent and motive, on the practical matter of playing objectives beat by beat, according to an analysis of the through line and superobjective of the play. Meisner trained his students to focus on others on stage, to respond honestly to 'the moment' as created anew through stage contact each night between actors. He distrusted excessively internalised techniques such as 'emotion memory' and 'sense memory' – and any techniques which unduly emphasised self-involvement at the expense of contact. His actors had inner life, but they were not inhibited externally. What Mamet admired most about Meisner was that what he taught was 'absolutely practicable'.[6]

During his college years, Mamet added to his South Side tough-guy credentials by taking a variety of blue-collar jobs while gaining further theatrical experience. In summer 1966 he worked for the merchant marine on the Great Lakes, which he would draw on for *Lakeboat*. In summer 1967, he joined Maurice Chevalier's company in Montreal as a specialty dancer. In summer 1968, he was in summer stock at Greenport, on the tip of Long Island. Goddard students could also work during a winter break period of two months. He began to write during this period and showed some of his early work to Mark Ryder, a choreographer at Goddard, who told him not to worry too much about form and structure – that would be a job for critics.[7] His BA thesis in English literature, awarded in spring 1969, was for an original Second City style revue called *Camel*.

For the next few years, Mamet shuttled between the hand-to-mouth existence of a young professional theatre worker and stints of acting–teaching in college. On graduation, he returned to Montreal and became a member of a professional company based on McGill University. He appeared in Pinter's *The Homecoming* and a version of *Alice in Wonderland*. He then returned to Chicago and began to drive a cab. He worked for nearly a year as office-manager for a dubious real estate firm on Peterson Avenue in North Side Chicago, a world he would later bring galvanically to life in *Glengarry Glen Ross*. In autumn 1970, he landed a one-semester appointment replacing a faculty member at Marlboro College in

Vermont as an acting-teacher. One of the job requirements
was to write a play that could be produced in workshop, so
he quickly formulated *Lakeboat*, which was duly presented
at Marlboro late in 1970. Early in 1971 he was back working
a variety of jobs in the Chicago area. In autumn 1971, he
was invited back to Goddard College to teach for a year.
With his students Steven Schachter and William H. Macy,
he formed a group called the St Nicholas Company, and
they performed early versions of *Sexual Perversity in
Chicago* and *The Duck Variations*. Enthused students saw
to it that he was invited back for a second year, and after the
first production he was given the title 'artist in residence'.
In autumn 1972 *The Duck Variations*, preceded by the
monologue *Litko*, was performed in Chicago at the New
Room of the Body Politic, a small store-front theatre on
Lincoln Avenue. These were the first Mamet plays to be
presented in his home city. In autumn 1973, Mamet again
moved back, to the Hotel Lincoln near the Old Town, and
made a living with theatre jobs when possible and other
jobs when necessary. He worked in a children's theatre
company, and performed in winter stock in various dinner
theatres in the Chicago area. Other jobs included selling
carpets on the 'phone and working as a busboy, clearing
tables, at the London House supper club.

In summer 1974, the Organic Theatre Company
presented a revised version of *Sexual Perversity in Chicago*
uptown at the Leo Lerner Theatre. The play deals with a
young love affair failing to withstand pressures from
masculinity myths, worldly-wise mentors and the urban
environment. It shocked some, delighted others, and
pulled in audiences in large numbers; and it gave Mamet
the cue to contact Schachter and Macy, who had gone to
California, and to reconstitute the St Nicholas Company as
the St Nicholas Players, with some new local members. In

November, *Sexual Perversity in Chicago* won Mamet his first Jefferson Award for the best new play of the Chicago season.

The St Nicholas Players got off to a shaky start, but later in the season took a turn for the better. The first production was Mamet directing Mamet: *Squirrels* (1974), a comedy about two writers locked in a mentor–protégé relationship. It intrigued some of the younger critics who had pegged Mamet as a man to watch after the success of *Sexual Perversity in Chicago*, but it did not draw audiences. Then, in February 1975, Mamet edited and directed O'Neill's first full-length play, *Beyond the Horizon* (1918), at the Grace Lutheran Church on West Baldwin Street. The reception was dismal. Christiansen has described how the group now resorted to desperate odd-jobbing and commissioned theatre work to keep going – Mamet himself took a job as girlie copy-editor at Hugh Hefner's *Oui* magazine. The group did a version of *The Canterbury Tales* at the Gurnee Renaissance 'faire', they presented Schachter's production of *A Midsummer Night's Dream* at the Oak Park Theatre Festival, and in June they opened a children's play by Mamet, *The Poet and the Rent*, which was enthusiastically received.

By the summer of 1975, Mamet felt a new tension about how he was spending his time and how his career was developing. The possibilities of becoming a nationally known playwright conflicted with his responsibilities as artistic director of the St Nicholas Players. 'I wished I could have done them both, to direct the company, and pursue my interests in New York, or even keep writing; it just didn't seem to be true.' There had been a disappointment in May when a showcase of *The Duck Variations* at St Clements in New York had been cancelled ten minutes before opening because of a dispute with Actors' Equity.

Mamet had been working on several plays; *Mackinac*, a play about Indians in North Michigan, had been presented by the Bernard Horwich Jewish Community Center in November 1974; and a year later they would do *Marranos* ('Swine'), a play about the persecution of the Jews during the Spanish Inquisition. More important was *American Buffalo*, which was completed by autumn 1975, as well as some of the vignettes which would later comprise *A Life in the Theatre*. Mamet decided not to do *American Buffalo* at his own theatre. Instead, he wanted it produced at the better-established Goodman. This theatre had existed as part of the Chicago Art Institute since 1925 and had a reputation as a solidly established professional regional theatre noted for its productions of classics and its drama school. He gave the play to Gregory Mosher, the young director of the Goodman's 'alternative' season, called the Stage Two, at the Ruth Dearborn Auditorium. By the time *American Buffalo* opened there in October, *Sexual Perversity in Chicago* had premiered in New York with *The Duck Variations* at the St Clements, directed by Albert Takazauckas, and it had been well received. The compelling new play – energetic yet practically 'actionless', simple on the surface yet layered with ironies – was a study of three small-time North Side hustlers plotting a coin-collection robbery from a junkshop. A significant number of critics regarded it as a fascinating, maddening or original work. Claudia Cassidy, doyenne of Chicago critics, epitomised what would become a common complaint about Mamet when she asked on WFMT radio: 'Does the Goodman Stage Two really believe that filthy language is a substitute for drama?'[8] The play did so well that, with one change of cast, it transferred to the new St Nicholas premises on Halstead Street and then was mounted by Mosher at the St Clements in New York with a new cast on 23 January. Meanwhile in Chicago the St Nicholas mounted a benefit revival of *Squirrels* on 7 and 8 January, and on the 9th presented a midnight showcase of a short Mamet play, *Reunion*, which had been written in 1973. The tension that Mamet had felt for months was finally resolved early in the New Year. Ostensibly because of some disagreement with his colleagues over the merits of a play being considered for production, Julian Barry's *Sitcom*, Mamet resigned the artistic directorship of the St Nicholas Theatre.

He now moved to New York. The St Clements *American Buffalo* production attracted the attention of Broadway producers Ed Lansbury and Joseph Baruh. On 16 June, *Sexual Perversity in Chicago* and *The Duck Variations* opened off-Broadway at the Cherry Lane Theatre and were to run there for 273 performances.[9] In the latter part of 1976, Mamet won a second Jefferson Award for *American Buffalo*, an Obie for that play and the Cherry Lane double-bill, a grant for children's theatre playwriting from the New York State Council for the Arts, a Rockefeller Grant, and a CBS Fellowship in Creative Writing to be partly spent in residence at Yale, where he would also teach one day a week.

1977 was a remarkable year for Mamet. He continued his professional association with Mosher and the Goodman by solving a repertory crisis in Stage Two with *A Life in the Theatre*, a deceptively episodic piece about two actors' lives in a regional theatre. It was a surprise hit on 3 February. The house gave Mamet a standing ovation, and the play received glowing reviews. Then came the Broadway opening of *American Buffalo* at the Barrymore Theatre on 16 February, directed by Ulu Grosbard, with Kenneth McMillan, John Savage and Robert Duvall. Reviews were mixed and the play had a moderate run for Broadway of

135 performances, but critics generally agreed that a new, individual voice had arrived and the play won the New York Drama Critics Circle Award. The same month, a short play called *All Men are Whores: An Inquiry* opened at the Yale Cabaret Theatre. On 11 May came the St Nicholas premiere of *The Water Engine*, directed by Steven Schachter. This was an adaptation of a radio play written the year before. Mamet uses the play-within-a-play format as actors in a 1934 radio studio create an 'American fable' of an inventor's duel with unscrupulous business interests. The children's play *The Revenge of the Space Pandas* was premiered by the St Clements State Co. in June. In October, *Reunion* was presented at the Yale Repertory Theatre with a new curtain-raiser, *Dark Pony*. Six days later, *A Life in the Theatre* opened at the Theatre de Lys off-Broadway, directed by Gerald Gutierrez, with Ellis Rabb and Peter Evans as the actors, and eventually played for 288 performances. In Chicago on 11 November, Mamet himself directed Patti LuPone and Peter Weller in his new play, *The Woods*, for the St Nicholas Theatre. It is a two-character play about lovers who interact in the isolation of a summer house and try to come to terms with themselves and their relationship. On 1 December, Mamet had his first important production abroad when *Sexual Perversity in Chicago* and *The Duck Variations* opened in London's West End at the Regent Theatre. The reception was lukewarm; some British critics were irritated by misleading advertising, including bare female buttocks on the poster, and the production only lasted until 14 January.[10] This exhaustive offering of highly varied work left critics frequently enthusiastic but at a loss how to pigeonhole Mamet. The whirlwind year was capped four days before Christmas by Mamet's marriage to Lindsay Crouse, the actress daughter of Pulitzer Prize-winning

playwright Russel Crouse. She had played in the double-bill at Yale, and *Dark Pony* is dedicated to her.

The next two years were marked by some professional setbacks which were devastating to Mamet at the time, but which led to a new career in screenwriting. *The Water Engine* proved a hit in New York at Joseph Papp's Public Theatre in its 'cabaret' format, but lasted only sixteen performances when moved uptown with the curtain-raiser *Mr Happiness* to the Plymouth Theatre on 16 March. The much-awaited New York opening of *The Woods* on 25 April 1979 proved a failure; Ulu Grosbard's production for Joseph Papp closed after only thirty-three performances. Worst of all was the trauma at the Goodman Theatre with *Lone Canoe, or, The Explorer.* This much-touted play with music, intended as the climax of the Goodman's mainstage season, opened in Chicago before the audience which included sixty critics at the American Theatre Critics' Association Convention on 24 May 1979. Based on a Jack London story, it is about an explorer faced with a decision whether to return to London or to remain 'lost' in the far north in his new home among the Indians. The play was panned and parodied by Second City, and even its director Mosher regarded the production as a spectacular failure. In the autumn, however, Mamet was hired by Bob Rafaelson, a Hollywood director, to write a screen adaptation of James M. Cain's *The Postman Always Rings Twice*, and enthusiastically responded to Rafaelson's crash course in screenwriting. The film was shot in spring 1980 with Jack Nicholson and Jessica Lange as the obsessed lovers.

In spite of setbacks, there were important consolidations of earlier theatrical successes in these two years as well. Very important was the British premiere of *American Buffalo*, directed by Bill Bryden, with Jack Shepherd as

Teach, at the smallest of the National Theatre's houses, the
400-seat Cottesloe, on 28 June 1978. This production made
far more impact than the short-lived double-bill earlier at
the Regent. Mamet had been named associate director of
the Goodman Theatre when Mosher had become full
artistic director in 1978; the failure of *Lone Canoe* was
somewhat balanced by a very successful revival of *A Life in
the Theatre* the following October. A fruitful connection
with off-Broadway's Circle in the Square Repertory began
with a production of *The Poet and the Rent* in May 1979,
and with Mamet himself directing Lindsay Crouse and
Michael Higgins the following October in a well-received
Reunion and *Dark Pony* – though he included a third
playlet, *The Sanctity of Marriage*, which was not so well
liked. *A Life in the Theatre* was nationally televised by
WNET on 27 June with Rabb and Evans repeating their
off-Broadway roles; and a British production was directed
by Alan Pearlman at the Open Space Theatre in July.

The three years 1980–2 culminated with a new film, *The
Verdict*, adapted for the director Sidney Lumet from a
novel by Barry Reed, and a new play, *Edmond*, which
opened at the Goodman on 14 June 1982, directed by
Mosher. The play and the film had strong thematic
similarities and focused on a single character's passage
through a blighted, morally ambivalent world to
enlightenment. *The Verdict*, which opened in December
1982, featured Paul Newman in the role of the lawyer hero
and was well received. It won Mamet an Oscar nomination
in the best-adaptation category early the following year.
Edmond was enthusiastically received in Chicago but
received mixed notices when it opened in New York at the
off-Broadway Provincetown Playhouse on 27 October
1982, and was panned by Frank Rich, the powerful critic of
the *New York Times*. It played for only seventy-seven

performances, but it won Mamet his second *Village Voice* Obie.

During this time, revival and reassessment of some of Mamet's earlier work increased. In April 1980, the Milwaukee Repertory Theatre, under John Dillon's direction, staged a tightened and revised version of *Lakeboat*; this deals with a student's summer sojourn as crew replacement aboard a merchant marine ship on the Great Lakes. The play was a success, and was done later at the Long Wharf Theatre in New Haven, the Goodman, and elsewhere. In October 1980, a Long Wharf revival of *American Buffalo*, directed by Arvin Brown with Al Pacino as Teach, began a long career in many guises which would take it to off-Broadway in 1981 and Broadway in 1983. *The Woods*, however, failed to please many New York critics the second time around when Mamet tried to re-create his Chicago production with the original cast in May 1982 at the Second Stage.

Mamet's career from early 1983 has been dominated by the Pulitzer Prize-winning *Glengarry Glen Ross*. It has been Mamet's most acclaimed play, though before it was staged Mamet had doubts about its unusual structure. It deals with a tough, all-male milieu he knew well – that of Chicago real-estate salesmen selling out-of-state unimproved land to the unwary. A reading of the play he arranged dissatisfied him, and for the first time he asked advice from a playwright he admired. Harold Pinter told him that all the play needed was a production, and duly arranged one with Peter Hall, the artistic director of the National Theatre of Great Britain. So it was that *Glengarry Glen Ross* was the first Mamet play to be premiered abroad, with the same director, leading actor and theatre – Bryden, Shepherd and the Cottesloe – as in the 1978 English production of *American Buffalo*. The opening on

21 September 1983, was highly praised. The play won the SWET Award in January 1984, and the American premiere, directed by Mosher, took place at the Goodman Theatre on 6 February. With one cast change, the production transferred to Broadway's John Golden Theatre on 25 March 1984. The reviews were enthusiastic. There had been almost no advance ticket sale, and the play lost money for its first two weeks. After it was known that Mamet had won the Pulitzer, takings jumped 30 per cent, and the play did not close on Broadway until 17 February 1985, after 378 performances. It then went on a coast-to-coast road tour which lasted until the end of the year.[11]

Mamet's other work at this time included shorter plays, sometimes very unusual in form; essays; adaptations of two European plays; and teaching. Though some critics charged that *Glengarry Glen Ross* was a return to earlier-won ground, much of this other work clearly indicates artistic advances. The smaller plays included *Five Unrelated Pieces*, presented at the New York Ensemble Theatre in May 1983; *The Disappearance of the Jews*, a one-act two-character play, presented on a triple-bill at the Goodman the same month; *The Dog*, *Film Crew* and *Four A.M.*, performed at Jason's Park Royal in New York the following July; *Vermont Sketches*, performed at the Ensemble in May 1984; *The Spanish Prisoner*, premiered with *The Shawl* in April 1985 by the New Theatre Company in Chicago; and two equally adventurous short plays broadcast on Chicago radio in March 1985 – *Goldberg Street* and *Cross Patch*. The adaptations were *Red River* (from Pierre Laville's *Le Fleuve rouge*), performed on the Goodman Theatre main stage in May 1983; and a two-hour streamlining of a literal translation of Chekhov's *The Cherry Orchard* by Peter Nelles, which inaugurated the New Theatre Company of the Goodman Theatre in March

1985. The screenplays were *Malcolm X*, *Things Change* (written with Shel Silverstein), *The Untouchables*, written for Paramount in 1985, and *The Tell*, filmed by Orion in June 1986. In 1983 and for the next two years, Mamet and William H. Macy participated in what Mamet called the Practical Aesthetics Workshop, a summer course on acting held at New York University. Out of this group the Atlantic Theatre Company was founded, which now operates in Chicago and Montpelier.

Mamet's life is now one in which he can realise all of this professional activity in a vital and fruitful manner. He lives in a restored farmhouse in rural Vermont with his wife and young daughter Willa, though they also have a New York apartment. Much of his writing is done in a small cabin on a grassy knoll behind the Vermont house. It seems that in future less new Mamet work will be done in Chicago. The St Nicholas Theatre went defunct in 1981, after several years of decline following the departure of its founders. Mosher started the New Theatre Company as an adjunct of the Goodman Theatre in 1985, but left the following summer when he was appointed artistic director of the Lincoln Center Theatre. It was in the Mitzi Newhouse Theatre of Lincoln Center that the premiere took place on 24 December 1985 of a double-bill of *Prairie du Chien* (1979) and *The Shawl*. The longer play, *The Shawl*, concerns a professional 'mystic' torn between loyalties to a male lover and a female client. The play was better received in its original Chicago New Theatre production in April than it was in New York.

2
'A Sense of
Moral Dismay'

In 1977, Mamet's work was characterised by Mel Gussow as having an irrepressible 'comic impulse, a heightened social consciousness, and a sense of moral dismay'.[1] The last quality is especially significant. It is a result of the constant sense of dichotomy, dialectic and paradox which abounds in the plays, whether they end 'negatively' with destructive forces predominant, or in a more 'positive' vision of contact.

Mamet's essay 'First Principles' begins with a typical example of this kind of opposition: 'The proclamation and repetition of first principles is a constant feature of life in our Democracy. Active adherence to these principles, however, has always been considered un-American.'[2] The plays resonate with other examples. Pious maxims of American liberalism derived from frontier myths are invoked by seedy crooks to justify morally culpable ends. Characters brimming over with energy apply their drives to the wrong goals. Men with a gift for the cut-and-thrust of talk, and with the imagination to fashion mesmerising stories, use these abilities to block rather than promote their ability to know themselves and others. Eager to experience genuine love, men and women none the less cast their sex partners into reductive scenarios which prevent it. Eager to bond with others in friendship and loyalty, men nevertheless manipulate, cheat and exploit each other into states of isolation. The characteristic attitude engendered in the audience is indeed one of moral dismay, and it has Brechtian, dialectical implications. Why, we ask, do men and women act this way, when they should have the capacity to act otherwise? At times in Mamet they do act otherwise, and the audience's moral dismay is suddenly lifted with the unexpected clear light of approval.

Mamet's moral vision as unveiled in his plays, his demonstration of how often his characters fall short of their potential, has been developed and bolstered from a variety of sources: Aristotle, the Stoics, Freud, Karl Marx, Bruno Bettelheim, Joseph Campbell, the Chicago turn-of-the-century economist Thorstein Veblen, Tolstoy and Stanislavsky.

The vision is not 'political' in the standard sense, though Mamet has spoken up boldly on a number of political issues, from America's involvement in Nicaragua to the greed of developers in wanting to demolish some of New York's finest old theatres. Politics he has called the 'last refuge of the unimaginative',[3] and his plays have not called for a changed political system or revolution on a grand scale. Many of the plays posit a societal malaise that no changed political system could alleviate – so much so that he has been called a pessimist and an apolitical playwright by some critics. He disapproves of plays in which political

message-making is paramount, whether the 'politics' relate
to aesthetic approaches or to governmental systems; and he
contrasts such propaganda with the artistic urge, which
involves free expression regardless of consequences. He
has expressed his conviction that apocalypse is just around
the corner – but, in a typical qualification, he has said that
the theatre is a place in which intent and will can be
celebrated, and that no subject is a fit subject for drama
which does not involve a possible choice.[4] The implication
is that, no matter how apathetic society has become and no
matter how near apocalypse looms, men and women can
still make choices about how to live their lives; that they can
work positively to find solutions to their own social and
personal dilemmas; that strong will and intent can bring
changes. His position is perhaps not so far from that of the
revolutionary Marat in Weiss's *Marat/Sade* (1964): 'The
important thing / is to pull yourself up by your own hair / to
turn yourself inside out / and see the whole world with fresh
eyes.'[5]

One of Mamet's premises is that man has delegated
personal responsibility for actions to various institutions.
In 1977, he said

> People are neurotic and whole nations are neurotic
> because they fail to recognize their true natures.
> Individuals fail to accept responsibility for what
> happens to them. . . . Marx said we all have an innate
> capacity to do good, to be loving, to be creative, but we
> alienate those capacities from ourselves. Rather than say
> this about ourselves we assign power and responsibility
> to our institutions, to the church, to the state, to
> medicine.[6]

Institutions are feared, because they are faceless and

impersonal – but approved, because they can justify acts which individuals would never wish to claim as their own.

People fall back on playing roles created for them by a consumer society and become items in a system of commodity exchange – counters in business, sexual and superficial 'interpersonal' transactions. American frontier myths and principles of Lockean liberalism have lost any moral value they might once have had, have become institutionalised and debased pieties, and in that form can be used to abnegate personal responsibility.[7] The pace and dislocation fostered by modern urban life have further intensified a reliance on 'received' social roles which keep people from understanding themselves. People have no time to develop an inner life, a sense of personal values which can shore them up against the negative coercions of society. There are no efficacious rituals and ceremonies to help people develop such values. Mamet has said,

> We are spiritually bankrupt – that's what's wrong with this country. We don't take Sundays off. We don't pray. We don't regenerate our spirit. These things aren't luxuries. . . . The spirit has to be replenished. There has to be time for reflection, introspection, and a certain amount of awe and wonder.[8]

Because most of his characters have little sense of such an inner life, they have no way of making real contact with each other.

Contact ripening into communion is the salvation that Mamet hints at. The kind of interconnectedness between people that Tolstoy postulated in 'What is Art?' and that Stanislavsky held up as the duty of the actor to help propagate in *An Actor Prepares* Mamet believes the theatre can help effect in society. In 1978 he said that 'My plays are about people trying to become connected. People who are confused . . . trying to do good. . . . But no one knows *how*. No one ever quite makes it.'[9] In Mamet's world, the attempt to make contact is crucial; in some of the early plays and more often in the later ones, contact is sometimes actually made.

Mamet's dialogue has been given critical attention sometimes at the expense of its context – but it is a major means to indicate any character's self-awareness and moral insight, and so his chance for connection with others. Mamet's most flashy and colloquially grounded dialogue – as demonstrated in, especially, the Chicago-based plays *American Buffalo*, *Sexual Perversity in Chicago* and *Glengarry Glen Ross* – usually comes from the mouths of characters possessed by the negative coercions of social form. In Mamet, the greatest masters of effective 'blah' are those who are most lost, deluded and compromised. They are often the greatest victims of their own 'gift', for it is a barrier to knowing themselves or others, a grab-bag of hand-me-downs, an imposed idiom which derives mostly from social masks and social role-playing. Indeed, the verbal energy and fluency of these characters is an inverse barometer of their ability to formulate their own personalised language. They often use their talk as an aggressive mask to hide behind, to dominate or manipulate others or to reduce their listeners to the stereotyped sexual roles they have provided for them in their own scenarios. Such talk inhibits rumination about their past experience, so that the audience feels limited in its knowledge of them. Some obtuse critics complained of the limitations of 'flat' or 'undeveloped' characters. That, of course, is the point – and characteristic of much drama written in the early 1970s which examined the limitations of social role-playing.

Especially in the 'Chicago' plays, the verve of the

dialogue which comes from the impulse to self-assertion
and justification has the secondary function of typecasting
various 'associates' into cartoons. 'Stories' about these
associates thus further flatten out the characters'
perceptions of their world – and sharpen the audience's
comic dismay at their reductive vision. A good example,
furnished by *American Buffalo*, epitomises Mamet's skill at
dialogue composition. A gentle encounter between Don,
owner of the junkshop, and his surrogate son Bobby is
interrupted by Teach, who storms in furious at two female
'associates' who have beaten him at poker the night before:

TEACH. I'm gonna order just a cup of coffee.

DON. Right.

TEACH. So Grace and Ruthie's having breakfast, and
they're done. *Plates* . . . *crusts* of stuff all over . . . So
we'll shoot the shit.

DON. Yeah.

TEACH. Talk about the *game* . . .

DON. . . . yeah.

TEACH. . . . *so* on. Down I sit. 'Hi, hi.' I take a piece of
toast off Grace's plate . . .

DON. . . . uh-huh . . .

TEACH. . . . and she goes 'Help yourself.'
Help myself.
I should help myself to half a piece of toast it's four
slices for a quarter. I should have a nickel every time
we're over at the game, I pop for coffee . . . cigarettes
. . . a *sweet roll*, never say word.
'Bobby see who wants what.' Huh? A fucking *roast
beef* sandwich. (*To* BOB) Am I right? (*To* DON) Ahh,
shit. We're sitting down, how many times do I pick up
the check? But (No!) because I never go and make a
big *thing* out of it – it's no big thing – and flaunt like

'This one's on me' like some bust-out asshole, but I naturally assume that I'm with friends, and don't forget who's who when someone gets *behind* half a yard or needs some help with (huh?) some fucking rent, or drops enormous piles of money at the track, or someone's *sick* or something . . .

DON (*To* BOB). This is what I'm talking about.

TEACH. Only (and I tell you this, Don). Only, and I'm not, I don't think, casting anything on anyone: from the mouth of a Southern bulldyke asshole ingrate of a vicious nowhere cunt can this trash come. (*To* BOB) And I take nothing back, and I know you're close with them.

Such dialogue was seized on by enthusiastic critics as the key to Mamet's importance and individuality. There was early controversy about whether the dialogue in the first plays was demotic and naturalistic, or stylised. In fact, it is both: a brilliant, heightened distillation of blue-collar Chicago talk, tuned through an ear acutely sensitive to the idiom and rhythm of that talk as it exists in actuality. The best analysis is still Ross Wetzsteon's in his early *Village Voice* article.[10] He draws attention to the heady combination of euphemisms, approximations, ellipses; omissions of linking words and phrases in some sentences, and additions of unnecessary words and phrases in others; the startling juxtaposition of the stilted and the profane, the 'high' and 'low' levels of language; the feel for dynamics of spoken rhythm; and at times the 'utter clarity of total grammatical chaos'. All of these characteristics are illustrated in the quoted passage. For Mamet, the actual stress patterns and the effect of spoken dialogue are vital, and he will often alter lines after he has heard them spoken by actors. It has been pointed out that the lines often fall into iambic pentameter. Teach's entrance line in *American Buffalo* – 'Fuckin' Ruthie, fuckin' Ruthie, fuckin' Ruthie, fuckin' Ruthie, fuckin' Ruthie' – is an example.

But critical fascination with the dialogue, especially in the first plays to be done in New York, led to an overvaluation of it – something that Mamet encouraged. He told Wetzsteon,

> My main emphasis is on the rhythm of language – the way action and rhythm are identical. Our rhythms describe our actions – no, our rhythms *prescribe* our actions. I became fascinated – I still am – by the way, the way the language we use, its rhythm, actually determines the way we behave, more than the other way around.

Certainly one can agree with the suggestion that socially conditioned language influences the behaviour and thought of many Mamet characters – but Mamet, in stating that 'language creates behavior' comes perilously close to saying that language cues intent and motive. In any case, he gave several critics the lead for advancing the idea that conventional external action in his plays had been replaced by 'language as action'. Michael VerMeulen and Robert Storey argued, for instance, that language, because it exists as a method of motivating action, is itself an action; and 'Mamet's characters . . . *are* their language; they exist insofar as – and to the extent that – their language allows them to exist. Their speech is not a smokescreen but a *modus vivendi.*'[11] Taken thus, the 'language equals action' idea becomes eccentric and rests very rockily on its foundation in Stanislavsky.

Around the time of the first production of *The Woods*, the critics became aware that Mamet's work also included a different group of plays in which the virtuosities of street-smart talk were not so apparent, plays which offered a clumsier, fissured speech with less aggressively rhythmic cadences. This dialogue was sometimes formally set in verse; it seemed stilted because of its lack of contractions; it was apt to slide into inarticulate, sometimes 'ineffective', silences, as in this passage from *The Woods*:

> RUTH. It's nice.
> NICK. Yes.
> RUTH. All *warm* . . .
>   *Look* at that!
>   The wind howls and howls, but you're warm.
> NICK. I'd sit here.
> RUTH. Yes.
> NICK. And think about things like that.
> RUTH. Would you? (*Pause.*) What things?
> NICK. You know.
>   *Pause.*
> RUTH. Tell me.
> NICK. Homes and things.
> RUTH. When the storms blew.
> NICK. Yes.
> RUTH. What about them?
> NICK. Living in them. Being warm.

Earlier, Mamet had used a more introversive kind of speech occasionally, and at such times he would put it in parentheses, which served to signal a 'momentary change to a more introspective regard' on a character's part. But later that stage direction occurred less and less often and finally not at all, though it was sometimes replaced by the simpler indication '*to self*'. This may have been a sign that, in Mamet's new kind of dialogue, the barriers between inner- and outer-directed talk have become more uncertain. But more puzzling to some critics was the formality, the hesitancy, and the lack of idiomatic qualities in this kind of dialogue. Was Mamet losing his ear? And consequently his special voice?

What is now apparent is that the more 'positive' implications of Mamet's moral vision – the potential in his characters for introspection, self-realisation and hence contact with others – are enshrined not in glib, 'effective' speech, but in that of the other kind. The potential for positive contact tends to be manifested less in the text of dialogue than in nuance, implication, pause and silence; and in the will and intent that the rhythm of words, more than the word-choice itself, portends. Many of Mamet's characters distrust words, have a need, which goes unmet, for a genuine language of positive communication. Mamet has stated in an essay that we 'don't trust words. Our anger is so great that we can only blurt and stammer. You know?'

But immediately the opposing proposition is held out: 'things do mean things', and 'there is a way things are irrespective of the way we *say* things are'.[12] Mamet shows certain characters aware of this, trying hesitantly to reconstitute words into a vehicle for communion. For example, at the climax of *The Woods*, Ruth tries to force Nick through physical blows into using such a language. And other characters, passing through the deconstruction of a 'received' language and beyond introspection, awe and wonder, begin to find it.

It is difficult to talk of Mamet's 'development' as a playwright, and deceptive to deal with the plays on a chronological basis of writing or production. Analysis of Mamet's formal strategies as a playwright can be based on whether or not the characters are capable of realising at least partly their potential for interconnectedness. The dialogue is a major signpost of this capability, but it is grounded in other dramaturgical elements. From early on in Mamet's work, plays of a more optimistic implication coexist with plays which elicit a full measure of his moral dismay.

Mamet has written of his great awareness in recent years of the satisfactions of 'plot', but Bigsby has rightly warned that, even when present in Mamet, the old-fashioned linear plot and the observance of the unities of time, place and action are often ironies.[13] One could go further and state that traces of such conventional plots are just a carapace for a more significant alternative structure underneath – a structure determined by social interrelationship, not conventional dramatic event, in which 'beats' are determined by interpersonal negotiation, drives to bonding or one-upmanship. This is true of *American Buffalo*, *Lakeboat*, *The Woods* and *The Shawl*. In *Glengarry Glen Ross*, conventional 'plot' becomes more important, but it too is a red herring for a more significant underlying structure of interrelationship between characters. Observance of the unities in several of these plays is ironic in that it points up the slightness of the plots that the unities frame; but, conversely, many of Mamet's more 'episodic' plays are not as fractured on stage as they appear to be on the page. In production, the structure which the plays assume has often been one of a filmic fluidity which emphasises disturbing juxtapositions of events. This sometimes implies a societal determinism which hypnotically conjoins people, times and places not logically or causally related.

When he has talked of 'plot' in recent years, Mamet has often meant the kind of narrative 'fairytale' or 'fable' promulgated by Bruno Bettelheim. His concept of a good play as a kind of 'myth' appealing to the dream-life of the audience partly derives from Bettelheim's description of a 'fairytale' as a non-didactic, symbolic story from which the audience is left to draw its own conclusions.[14] He has also been influenced by the archetypal mythic pattern of departure, initiation and enlightment of a hero-figure as analysed through international myth and legend by Joseph Campbell in *The Hero with a Thousand Faces*. Mamet frequently incorporates such narrative patterns both into the structure of whole plays and as 'stories' told by characters within plays. This strategy is specially prominent in several major plays from 1977 on: *The Woods*, *The Water Engine*, *Lone Canoe* and *Edmond*. Mamet believes in the theatre's power to educate and enlighten, and he endorses Tolstoy's and Stanislavsky's belief that the theatre can achieve this function if it deals with subject-matter that the ordinary man can understand and empathise with. Mamet admires those plays which are essentially allegories, modern 'fairytales' which tread an astute path between excessive naturalism on the one hand and presentational stylisation on the other. He has said, 'The dramatic experience concerned with the mundane may inform but it cannot release; and one concerned essentially with the *esthetic politics* of its creators may divert or anger, but it cannot enlighten.'[15]

Whereas certain characters especially in the earlier plays tend to be verbally ebullient, this is no indication of a fully detailed naturalistic characterisation. Mamet distrusts assumptions that his characters have a life outside the play. Deriving his line of reasoning partly from Bettelheim, he does not believe that fully 'illustrated' characterisation in a play is either desirable or necessary. This is specially evident in the later plays, where his concept of characterisation falls into close accord with that of plot as 'fairytale'. In 1981 he wrote that excessively specifying character traits – what he calls 'characterising' – only

encourages the audience to approach the play as critics
rather than as participants. In increasing specificity in
characterisation, a playwright inhibits identification: 'to
characterize the people or scene, is to take time from the
story, which is to weaken the story'.[16]

Mamet's concern for 'minimalism' has increased in
recent years. The vigorous paring-down of words is
especially apparent in the recent *Edmond*, *Glengarry Glen
Ross* and *The Shawl*. Acting, direction and design should
all consist of that bare minimum necessary to set forth the
action. The settings, like the characterisation, have tended
to become more severely selective, so that they often strike
the audience as metaphors rather than environments.

If one were to generalise about Mamet's overall strategy
as a playwright, one would say that he aims at a selective
realism, with strongly allegorical overtones, in plays in
which the essential and representative features of action
and character are stressed. It is arguable that, in some plays
in which the fable identification is strong, the sense of
moral dismay is vitiated – identification works against a
Brechtian degree of detachment in which the moral dismay
can manifest itself. This latter tone of slight 'alienation' is
elicited by Mamet's most characteristic plays. It is
arguable, too, that the allegorical implications most
powerfully emerge when Mamet is least self-conscious
about their importance, and when they are embedded in
just the right amount of 'characterising' overlay, just
enough detail to touch up a spareness that is too schematic.
This applies to plays such as *Reunion*, *Lakeboat*, *The Water
Engine* and *Glengarry Glen Ross*. Robert Brustein has said
about the latter play, for instance, that it is 'so precise in its
realism that it transcends itself and takes on reverbernt
ethical meanings'.[17]

3
Business

In all of Mamet's plays, the spirit of one-upmanship lies in wait to subvert contact between people. In two of his most powerful plays, this destructive spirit wins out.

There are many similarities between the early *American Buffalo* and the more recent *Glengarry Glen Ross*. They have all-male casts and deal with particularly male pressures and social dynamics; they are set in Chicago and are suffused with the street idiom and driving energy of that city; the dialogue is more prominent than usual; the scenic metaphor of a 'trashed' workplace forms a significant comment on the action; the main characters trap themselves as they become impaled on one precipitate, ill-considered action; a potential friendship between 'partners' is subverted by competitive one-upmanship and the forces it unleashes.

There is one more similarity too: these plays have been Mamet's most commercially and critically popular, and they are the only two of his plays to date which have enjoyed notably long Broadway runs. *American Buffalo* has had the more complicated production history. The 1977 Broadway production by Ulu Grosbard had only a modest run, but the revival directed by Arvin Brown, with Al Pacino as Teach, played first at the Long Wharf Theatre in New Haven in 1980, then at the Circle in the Square off-Broadway in 1981 and 1982, and finally came to Broadway in 1983. This proved that the play could work in quite different interpretations: the first emphasised claustrophobic violence, the second comic irony. The proof confirmed an important place for the play in modern American drama. *Glengarry Glen Ross*, after early doubts by Mamet, had an uncomplicated and linear string of successes initiated by the London premiere and crowned by the Pulitzer Prize.

Mamet has said of *Glengarry Glen Ross* that it is about a society based on business, a 'society with only one bottom line: How much money you make'.[1] American capitalism creates the incentives and the context that drive the salesmen of *Glengarry Glen Ross*. But it also creates the petty crooks of *American Buffalo*: the detritus of those on the bottom rung of the ladder, the 'have-nots' who, according to Thorstein Veblen, make up a 'delinquent' society as sensitively aware of rank and status as the 'leisure aristocracy' of successful businessmen, and as prone to operate on the same principles to justify predatory action.[2] Mamet has said of *American Buffalo* that it deals with

> the predatory aspect of American life. The whole Horatio Alger myth in America is false. It's a play about honour among thieves and the myths this country runs on. . . . Calvin Coolidge once said 'The business of America is business.' The ethics of the business community is that you can be as predatory as you want within a structured environment.[3]

In both plays, 'business' is a catchword for principles of operation which the characters have inherited from a debased frontier code of enterprise and initiative – a code which, Mamet has suggested, initially arose only from the desire to get something for nothing.[4] It is the driving force in a pattern of interaction in which men are involved in competitiveness and shifting power allegiances, embroiled in oscillating admiration and envy; collusion and opposition; active support and aggressive enmity. All of this, of course, subverts the social ideal of interconnectedness between men. The linkage of the action to American 'business' principles is direct and organic in *Glengarry Glen Ross*. In *American Buffalo* it is more metaphorical, and for this reason a tone colour of ironic, comic dismay is closer to the surface. In *American Buffalo*, the 'businessmen' are Veblen's 'delinquents', crooks who are the denizens of a junk shop operated by one of them.

In outline, the plot is deceptively simple and seems to hinge on a crime which never takes place. Donny Dubrow, the owner, has been infuriated by a young professional customer whom he believes outmanoeuvred him in a transaction involving a buffalo-head nickel. He has set Bobby, a teenager he has befriended, to spy on the man's apartment and plans to get his own back by stealing his 'coin collection'. Teach, a twitchy crony, edges in on the scheme and persuades Don to drop Bobby from the heist. Then in Act II the whole plan collapses, nothing is done, and Teach smashes up the junkshop in an exorcism of violent frustration. But this 'plot' is only a carapace for a deeper, subtler structure based on units of 'social interaction' between the three men. Here, competitive manipulation based on 'business' principles is played out with explosive consequences.

The dialogue – chiefly Teach's dialogue – becomes the chief dramaturgical element in the play through which the fever of 'business' principles is ingested by the characters. Just before Don rounds on and physically attacks Teach in the climactic violence of the play, he accuses, 'You stiff this one, you stiff that one . . . you come in here, you stick this poison in me . . .'. The poison is injected verbally, in the compulsions of vivid talk which Teach chiefly fuels. It seems that Teach's notions of 'business' have been imbibed by Don before he even enters, and Don gently passes them on to Bob. Business is 'common sense, experience, and talent', but it is also 'People taking *care* of themselves.' Friendship is defined more vaguely: 'what you got to do is keep clear who your friends are, and who treated you like what. Or else the rest is garbage.'

The dialogue becomes much more prominent in itself the minute that Teach enters. Harold Clurman's remark that it is the 'language of people who have not yet arrived at the stage of integrated personality; they are void of coherent inner experience',[5] applies most of all to Teach. Bigsby has pointed out how Teach's speeches are full of statements hilariously undercut with ironies deriving from his real intent and situation; how his criminal aims are justified with moral pieties lifted out of the frontier myth and Locke-derived liberalism, exposing the dubiousness of both for modern America in the process.[6] The staple of Teach's definition of 'business' is 'free enterprise', which he characterises as 'The freedom . . . Of the *Individual* . . . To Embark on Any Fucking Course that he sees fit . . . In order to secure his honest chance to make a profit'; unaware of the built-in contradiction, he adds, 'The country's *founded* on this, Don.' Much of the dismay we feel when we watch the play stems from the fact that Teach apparently has no notion of the gap between the acts he wants to commit and the moral pieties he invokes to justify them. The irony is signalled by Mamet's capitalisations in the dialogue, which are an indication to the director to provide an equivalent italicisation in performance – this 'alienates' in Brechtian fashion the comic delusions of the character. There is even greater potential comic irony at the climax, where Teach blames the failure of the crime on the very lack of loyalty and support which he has subverted in order to exclude Bob from the deal and maximise his own chance of profit. At the same time as he tears apart the junkshop, he trots out capitalised pieties: 'There Is No Law./There Is No Right And Wrong./The World Is Lies. / There Is No Friendship. / Every Fucking Thing.' The banality of the final line here 'alienates' the premises of the foregoing rhetoric, a not-uncommon comic device in Mamet. Another dialogue device is Teach's creation of extended scenarios in which he typecasts others as predators, 'business' adversaries and enemies. A good example of this kind of paranoia through dialogue is the diatribe against Grace and Ruthie quoted in the last chapter. Teach's world is one in which everyone is the enemy, and the paranoia invades the world of the whole play. And, though Teach seems to realise that there is emptiness in life, he does not have insights into how he is implicated in this emptiness – as the salesmen of *Glengarry Glen Ross* do. Even as he yearns for contact, he compulsively creates circumstances which ensure that he will live his life in isolation.

Though not initiating the action, Teach is the catalyst determining the pattern of social interactions which works below conventional 'plot' elements and forms the play's true structure. Teach's major intention through the play is to gain the respect and approval of Don at the same time as he is driving home the business maxims which will exclude

Bob from the deal and justify personal betrayal. In spite of
Don's earlier announcement to Bob that 'You don't have
friends this life', it is plain that he and Bob share a
friendship, and that he is mentor to the boy. This nurturing
relationship is often hinted at through pauses and the
gentle rhythms of words which sometimes belie their overt
meaning. Teach notices this – and his driving pejoratives
about 'business' and 'free enterprise' are clearly designed
to undermine it. They reveal his own desire to displace Bob
in a positive relationship with Don.

Teach seems to envision the same kind of accord
between peers that Roma later, in *Glengarry Glen Ross*,
glimpses for himself and Shelly Levene. An implicit
condition in the accord is that each party has certain
professional skills or human qualities that the other lacks.
For a common goal to be reached – in this case, stealing
the 'coins' – these qualities have to function in a
complementary way. The goal could not be reached by one
man alone. So the bonding takes the form of a quasi-
business 'partnership' which involves mutual support and
respect and – unlike the relationships of teacher–pupil and
mentor–protégé – it involves a tacit admission of equality-
in-differences, even when the ages of the men are different. All of this is implicit in *American Buffalo*; it
becomes more explicit in later Mamet works, including
Glengarry Glen Ross and the screenplay *The
Untouchables*.

Act I is an intricate, causally related series of transactions
and power-plays which function as 'beats' manipulated
mostly by Teach. They form structural units which take the
place of more conventional dramatic action. Teach
persuades the older man to exclude Bob from the break-in
team, a betrayal justified by 'business' considerations, and
this proves seminal for everything which follows. Don

counters this concession on his part by evaluating Teach through the very same 'business' considerations, and finds him wanting as 'hit-man'. So he decides to bring in a third man, an arch-street operative named Fletcher, to give 'depth' to the team. Though he gets a taste of his own medicine, Teach has reluctantly to accept this as sound 'business'. According to Don, Fletcher is the kind of man who knows 'how to get in', and the sexual innuendo amusingly links 'business' competence with sexual potency. By the end of Act I, Teach has left the junkshop, jumping like a puppy dog for Don's approval, and trying to cement the illusion of their equal partnership in the enterprise.

In Act II, Mamet steps up the irony, and the director can choose to highlight it or submerge it more subtly in the rising tension of the action. There is a whole stew of dialectical contrasts. Teach is late for the 11 p.m. appointment to help carry out the break-in; we learn later that he has hocked his watch to buy a gun – ultimate symbol of potency – but he is initially reprimanded by Don for not knowing the time. Bob appears unexpectedly with a facsimile of the buffalo coin that initiated the plan. He wants to sell it back to Don at no profit to himself – but this act of simple loyalty cannot be taken at face value, especially by Teach, whose jealousy and paranoid suspicions are immediately aroused and fed to Don. The situation is made more tense, and more inherently ridiculous, by the fact that the supposedly so reliable Fletcher fails to arrive. Finally, Don is on the brink of giving Teach the nod as 'hit man,' the sign of approval that Teach most wants. At this point, Teach flashes his gun, ostensibly to protect himself against 'Public *officials . . . ax* murderers' who may 'go nuts'. But the approval is thwarted by another intrusion from Bob.

Bob's return initiates a cause-and-effect progression which results in an impulsive action by Teach; and this not only prevents the robbery from taking place but also precludes his achievement of any kind of 'partnership' with Don. Bob tells them that Fletcher has been mugged; primed by Teach, Don assumes that Bob is lying, that he and Fletcher have gone in ahead of them, and that the coin offered to Don was in fact the original nickel that initiated the whole plan. Don does not intervene as Teach grills Bob in mounting anger and finally smashes him on the side of the head with a hard object. This proves decisive: Bobby, bleeding from the head, must be taken to hospital at once. Don now lays the failure for the whole plan at Teach's door. He savagely beats Teach, rejecting him in doing so, whereas Teach masochistically confirms this rejection by ravaging the shop with a pig-sticker. When Bob confesses that the evidence on which the whole plan was based – that he saw the mark (intended victim) leaving his apartment for the weekend – was all fabricated, Teach sees his furious act as justified. At the end, he is taunted by seeing a reprise of the inchoate affection between Don and Bobby, but he is still pathetically eager for Don's approval.

The final rejection is underlined in dialogue which, in its halting rhythms and lack of 'effective' fluency, is always a sign in Mamet that masks have been dropped and that, for better or worse, vulnerabilities are being exposed. The disjunction in rhythm – especially as created by the three directions for 'pause' – imply the collapse of all possibilities for connection between the two men. It contradicts any hint of reconciliation implied by the meaning of the words:

TEACH. Are you mad at me?
DON. What?

TEACH. Are you mad at me?
> *Pause.*

DON. Come on.

TEACH. Are you?

DON. Go and get your car. Bob?

TEACH (*Pause*). Tell me are you mad at me.

DON. No.

TEACH. You aren't?

DON. No.
> *Pause.*

TEACH. Good.

DON. You go and get your car.

Teach then fishes for sympathy in another way, now like a child to a parent ('You fucking *child*', the salesman Roma later calls the errant office-manager in *Glengarry Glen Ross*, the ultimate epithet for incompetence in the business world). Don orders him about and, to save face, Teach acts like a clown, fashioning a paper hat for himself and looking at himself in the mirror: 'I look like a sissy' he comments, underlining his childish, denatured masculinity.

Many of Mamet's plays encapsulate a scenic metaphor in the title, and *American Buffalo* is one of the richest in this respect because, as Steve Lawson has pointed out, it includes three different references. There is the 'great beast reduced to a nickel; the mythical Old West dwindling into a junk shop; the guys who suspect they're being "buffaloed" by a young punk'.[7] But of course the buffalo nickel, through the original 'transaction' which led Don to think that he had been swindled, incites the action; and Bob's compensatory offer to Don sows the seeds of suspicion against him which contribute to the final explosion. More so than in most Mamet plays, therefore, a symbolic object is organically welded to action and structure.

The play, a little inconsequential at face value, leaves a provocative residue in the mind. A dialectical principle is again in operation. If the play is interpreted as 'realism' only, the action is practically non-existent, the characters small-time, the scope limited, underlined by the final scenic image of a stage full of trash doubly 'trashed'. But metaphorically the implications are considerable. It is partly *because* the action in the microcosm is so trivial that the validity of the macrocosm is so effectively questioned. *American Buffalo* confronts the validity of an entire national mystique, and the premises on which many enterprises and dreams of great moment are founded.

The major thematic concerns of *American Buffalo* are repeated in a more literal business milieu in *Glengarry Glen Ross*, with a similar outcome. Business principles again preclude a positive partnership; and the failure of the partnership is clinched by one precipitate, ill-considered action, which in turn releases a sequence of actions that prove incontrovertible.

The plot of *Glengarry Glen Ross* again centres upon a robbery, which this time does take place; and the chain of events that ensues, linked by cause and effect, comprises elements of a conventional 'rising action'. But this plot is still not as important as the 'submerged' pattern of interaction between the salesmen, the 'beats' limned by allegiances proposed or aborted, competition smoothed over or stepped up. The plot and this other pattern, however, prove to be increasingly interrelated as the play goes on. They are introduced in the three short two-handed scenes of Act I, all set in a Chinese restaurant where the salesmen gather and do business. All the scenes are self-contained, and appear to have little direct connection with each other. We learn that the men work for the same office and sell undeveloped land in Florida to gullible clients – the land has dubiously seductive names such as 'Glengarry Highlands' and 'Glen Ross Farms' – and that they are threatened by a sales competition in which the winner will get a Cadillac, the runner-up a set of steak-knives, and the losers will be fired. Scenes 1 and 3 suggest the pattern of interactions rather than the plot. In Scene 1, Shelly Levene, a sure loser in his fifties, desperately pleads with the office-manager Williamson to give him better leads, which are lists of customer prospects. He cajoles and then bribes, but to no avail. In Scene 3, Roma, the office star, draws a lonely drinker into a one-sided conversation based on Roma's stoic-tinged philosophy of doing 'those things which seem correct to me *today*'. This proves, in the scene's punch-line, to be integral to his sales approach. It is the intervening Scene 2 which initiates the plot. The runner-up Moss proposes to one of the losers, Aaronow, that he be the 'hit man' in an office break-in in which the firm's leads will be stolen and sold to a rival broker for a dollar a piece. Aaronow resists as the scene ends.

In the unbroken Act ii, the crime has taken place and the consequences play themselves out in the debris-ridden office. The plot assumes the contours of a whodunit as a detective takes the salesmen to an inner office at the back of the set offstage and grills them one by one. We are pretty sure Moss is guilty, but who actually broke in? Aaronow or someone else? Soon, however, the underlying pattern of social interaction between the salesmen takes on more sharpness and definition from the groundwork laid in Act i: Mamet reveals the affinity and regard between Roma and Levene. There are several intricate reversals, but near the climax Levene overreaches himself in supporting Roma over a lost sale and inadvertently exposes himself as the culprit. He is turned in. As in *American Buffalo*, the focal character is forever alienated from a 'partnership' with another because of one ill-considered act. But here the impact is greater, because Levene has committed a crime and his professional and personal life has been totally destroyed.

Again, the dialogue is a major means by which the characters prime themselves for action. For them, 'aggressive selling has become a means of defense and attack, of self-identification and of *being*', wrote Stanley Kauffman, and stressed that this is mainly accomplished through the dialogue, 'the intensification of (highly salty) vernacular from a means of communication into a grinding, almost unstoppable machine for onslaught'.[8] Unlike in the earlier play, the dialogue does not derive mostly from one character's energy, but seems to be shared in different ways by all the characters. It is the fuel which drives their efforts to succeed in the sales competition; it becomes the means whereby they put down, dominate or cajole colleagues, and drive home closing sales on their marks; and it is a mud-slide into criminal complicity. David Denby went so far as to call it a 'new mode of American speech – a language of pure intention, which darts ahead, anticipating objections and refusals'.[9] Dominant elements are phrases such as 'wait a second' and 'hold on a minute' and simultaneous and interrupted delivery, which are more prominent here than in the earlier play. Gone are the parentheses indicating 'introspective regard', and even the direction '*to self*' hardly occurs – the situations here do not allow for such moments.

In *American Buffalo* it was the interactions between Teach and Don which proved crucial for the outcome of the play; here the relationship between Roma and Levene is central in a somewhat different way. Through it, Mamet

brings home to the audience the loss in human fulfilment
that his focal character suffers because of his desperation
and short-sightedness. In Act I, Levene disparages Roma to
Williamson, in trying to get the latter's support. But in
Act II, Roma and Levene move toward greater personal
and professional accord – a 'partnership' which we find at
the climax has been aborted by Levene's criminal action.
But earlier the Roma–Levene relationship is firmly set
within the nexus of alternating support and rivalry that
operates among all the characters.

In the first scene of Act I, Levene hardly knows nor cares
that Roma might respect him. He is fighting for his
professional life, and Williamson is the man who can save
it. He evokes the camaraderie of support: 'Get on my side.
Go with me'; he insists that he is a person, not just a social
and professional role: 'I'm . . . don't look at the *board*,
look at *me*. Shelly Levene.' But Williamson is only
interested in cold cash for the leads – to be paid then and
there. When Levene can not deliver, the deal is off. Once
again, 'business' rules the roost, and Williamson emerges
as the play's most calculating and least sympathetic
character.

Early in Act II, Roma is furious at losing sales because of
the theft – but it is clear that he respects the old-fashioned
mystique of salesmanship and credits Levene for having
passed it on to him. Roma seems pleased when Levene
bursts in with news about a big sale – but Roma expresses
this in a put-down for Moss, who has just come out of a
gruelling interrogation by the detective. Roma criticises
Moss for not caring about Levene's elating success: 'Your
pal closes, all that comes out of your mouth is *bile*, how
fucked *up* you are . . .'; and Moss replies, '*Who's* my
pal . . . ? And what are you, Ricky, huh, what are you,
Bishop *Sheean*?' – a funny and significant exchange, for

Moss with cynical clarity assumes that in the competitive situation in which they are all placed there can be no 'pals', and that Roma is being a hypocrite for implying otherwise. As we know, Moss has already acted on that assumption.

Then begins a long, unbroken speech in which Levene tells Roma what making his sale was like, which illustrates 'The *old* ways . . . convert the motherfucker . . . *sell* him . . . *sell* him . . . *make him sign the check*', and it concludes with an apparent endorsement and show of respect from Roma.

> LEVENE.   . . . I *did* it. I *did* it. Like in the *old* days, Ricky. Like I was taught . . . Like, like, like I *used* to do . . . I did it.
> ROMA. Like you taught me . . .

Levene almost immediately has a chance to reciprocate this support. Roma spies outside his customer of the previous night, Lingk, coming to the office – obviously with second thoughts. Roma throws Levene a strategy, a role, and a word, 'Kenilworth', to be given on cue, and the men go into almost vaudevillian diversionary tactics in which Levene is a successful out-of-town executive who must be flown to O'Hare Airport, preventing Roma talking with Lingk at length. Roma's Cadillac and competition victory are at stake – Lingk's contract is only valid after a three-day grace period in which he has the right to change his mind. Roma tells him that this period will be up on the Monday, since the contract has not yet gone to the bank. Levene keeps up his role and his patter, and the strategy almost works. Roma is reassuring Lingk with a 'personal' line of argument; he rightly senses that Lingk misses male camaraderie and has mainly reneged because of his wife's bullying – and so he plays on this need, telling Lingk that he cares about him, not about the deal. But then Williamson unwittingly demolishes the entire effort by telling Lingk that his contract has indeed gone to the bank.

This is the structural equivalent of Bob's news about Fletcher in *American Buffalo* – it unleashes a series of events which brings about Levene's downfall. Because he is the culprit, he is the only one who knows for sure that Williamson is in fact lying to Lingk – his contract had not in fact gone to the bank but was stolen along with the leads. Roma merely assumes that Williamson has opened his mouth out of turn and heaps him with furious expletives – 'you fucking *child*' is the choice one he saves for last – before having to answer the cop's summons in the inner room.

The next scene, in which Levene in turn tears into Williamson in support of Roma and overreaches himself by showing Williamson that he knows he was lying, is one of Mamet's most brilliant. It is rich in irony and dialectical elements. Before he makes the fatal slip, Levene passionately defines the credo of true salesmanship to Williamson, a mere office-manager who has never been out on sales appointments, can never feel the thrills or even learn the skills of selling and the camaraderie it entails:

> LEVENE. You can't think on your feet you should keep your mouth closed. (*Pause.*) You hear me . . . You can't learn that in an office. Eh? He's right. You have to learn it on the streets. You can't *buy* that. You have to *live* it.

In defining his notion of partnership, he evokes the last frontier in words reminiscent of such a character as Pike, the leader in Sam Peckinpah's *The Wild Bunch*: 'Your partner . . . a man who's your "partner" *depends* on you

. . . you have to go *with* him and *for* him . . . or you're shit, you're *shit*, you can't exist alone . . . .'

There are two major ironies. The credo of support for Roma which Levene voices to Williamson he has already himself betrayed, by stealing Roma's contract along with the leads and so making it more likely for him to lose his victory, sale and Cadillac. His very vehemence betrays his guilt – a guilt of which he is well conscious. Secondly, in his vehemence he is guilty of the same professional shortcomings as he despises in Williamson: he cannot keep his own mouth shut when he is not thinking on his feet; and he has himself, in the first scene, tried to buy from Williamson a substitute for the professional skills that he now lacks. He pathetically falls short of his own professional standards, and is hoist with his own petard. Williamson finally turns the knife in the wound by refusing a last, desperate bribe, and by exposing the fact that Levene's much-vaunted sale has in fact been to eccentrics whose cheques habitually bounce.

Our moral dismay at Levene's action, mixed with sympathy for him stronger than any ever felt for Teach, intensifies in the play's final moments. When Roma emerges from his interrogation, he does not know that Levene has been found out as the guilty party, and he offers him a 'partnership' with a similar last-frontier colouration to that of Levene's own definition. He says that he and Levene are 'members of a dying breed', that they 'have to stick together' in a world of 'clock watchers, bureaucrats, officeholders', and there are things he could learn from Levene. There is a final irony, which Mamet and Mosher deleted from the American production for rhythmic reasons but which Mamet prefers to retain. Roma proposes to Williamson that he work with Levene as partner but take half his commissions. Just because Roma is promoting

Levene earlier does not preclude his betraying him here. And this perhaps indicates the evanescence of all and any relationships, including 'partnerships', which might be temporarily created among these salesmen.

But the climax of the play comes before this qualifying irony. Levene tries to respond to Roma's offer – and the response is shot through with the pathos inherent in the fact that he seems to realise all too late what he has betrayed. Levene desperately tries, and fails, to tell Roma this as the cop Baylen hustles him into the inner room and his final humiliation. It is reminiscent of the pathetic last overtures made by Teach to Don in *American Buffalo*, and it is a moment when the sureties of a glib, 'received' language fall away to expose the flummoxed vulnerability in a human being. It is not an entropic, Pinteresque effect: the subtext resonates with 'if only's' and undeclared regrets on Levene's part, and perplexed concern on Roma's. Neither can Levene salvage anything from what appears to be genuine professional respect on Roma's part. It is too late. The trap has closed on him.

> BAYLEN. Get in the goddamn room. (BAYLEN *starts manhandling* SHELLY [LEVENE] *into the room.*)
>
> LEVENE. Ricky, I . . .
>
> ROMA. Okay, okay, I'll be at the resta . . .
>
> LEVENE. Ricky . . .
>
> BAYLEN. 'Ricky' can't help you, pal.
>
> LEVENE. . . . I only want to . . .
>
> BAYLEN. Yeah. What do you want? You want to *what*? (*He pushes* LEVENE *into the room, closes the door behind him. Pause.*)

Mamet's attitude to his characters registers as more complex in *Glengarry Glen Ross* than in *American Buffalo*;

in the former it is more clearly a mixture of both condemnation and admiration. Michael Billington, reviewing the London production, summed it up well: 'Mamet . . . may not like the system; but he has a perverse, quirky admiration for the men who have to go out there and make it operate.'[10] The men may be operating on the edge of the law, but the language epitomises their compensating vitality. The language is the means by which they display their skills as spinners of convincing fictions; and Mamet admires these, because they are analogous to his skills as playwright. Like Teach, the salesmen have certain scenarios that put both their marks and their competition in derogatory roles and enhance their own self-images.

What separates the salesmen of this play from the petty hustlers of *American Buffalo* is that Mamet skilfully implies that the former both recognise the moral culpability of what they are doing and know that their 'business' masks are sometimes at odds with their inner aspirations and inclinations. In Moss's mouth Mamet puts a justification for the planned crime which conveniently absolves him from personal responsibility for criminal action. It is others, Moss argues, who in more prosperous times have garnered incommensurate profits from crooked real-estate deals, who have gone ahead to 'kill the goose' and have so forced him to do what he is about to do. The reasoning behind this, based on a long career in selling, is more calculatedly casuistic than the self-righteous pieties which Teach offers as excuses for his planned crime. And his admiration for the offstage broker Jerry Graff (equivalent of Fletcher in the earlier play) has a more solidly professional base: Graff has had the courage to do 'the *act*' of going into business for himself, and has made Moss's crime possible by agreeing to buy the leads. The other men all have selves peeping out occasionally from behind their masks. Roma can emerge from temporary setbacks to give support to men who are on the skids – Aaronow as well as Levene. We learn that Levene has supported a daughter through school by door-to-door selling, even though he always plays her as his last card, for sympathy, in his attempts to get Williamson's support. More so than is the case with *American Buffalo*, we get a sense of unrealised private lives just tantalisingly beyond the narrow, clear scope of professional activity that Mamet shows us. Bigsby says that Aaronow's refusal to implicate Moss in his offstage interrogation is evidence of loyalty to one of his kind, an instance of support in a tacit partnership of professionals that Levene has betrayed.[11]

The silences in the plays open up a dimension beyond the social. They suggest a metaphysical source for the crisis in decent human relations that is exposed. These plays thus move beyond the rational arena of a social problem play. The final lines of *Glengarry Glen Ross*, a counterpoint in which Aaronow confesses that he hates his job and Roma charges back to the restaurant for the next mark, suggest a complicity with something perverse in human nature, a collusion with both a faulty social system and a masochism in the personal psyche. ('We think of ourselves as victims, and so we become victims', says Joe Galvin in *The Verdict*.) But of course they also suggest the characters' gumption in continuing the perverse battle at any cost.

Though *Glengarry Glen Ross* is less comic and oblique in its implications about business than *American Buffalo*, and more directly moving, one of its greatest strengths is its objectivity. Incipient sentiment is balanced out by irony. The play was presented on Broadway at about the same time as a much-praised revival with Dustin Hoffman of Arthur Miller's *Death of a Salesman*. Comparisons were inevitable. And perhaps one of the most significant was that, whereas Miller's play is sometimes tendentious and sentimental, Mamet's is moral but never moralises. It thus successfully exemplified Mamet's own most important characteristic of a good play.

For all that, we are left in both *American Buffalo* and *Glengarry Glen Ross* with a pessimistic sense of the possibilities of human relationships. Mamet has said that 'there's really no difference between the *lumpenproletariat* and stockbrokers and corporate lawyers who are the lackeys of business. . . . Part of the American myth is that a difference exists, that at a certain point viciousness becomes laudable.'[12] Both the focal characters of these plays are victims of this assumption. Teach's jealousy and need to be the man who can 'get in' leads him to an action which prevents him ever achieving any 'partnership' with Don. Levene's crime, committed in desperation, betrays the values which might have given some authenticity to the 'partnership' with Roma. What is true of them is also true, to a lesser extent, of the other characters here. Their thraldom to the imperatives of 'business' at any cost has stunted them and prevents them from knowing either themselves or others.

4
Sex

If *American Buffalo* and *Glengarry Glen Ross* show possibilities for communion between men destroyed by 'business' pressures, *Sexual Perversity in Chicago* and *The Woods* show similar possibilities between men and women corroded by an even more complicated array of forces. There is social role-playing, which this time involves not only competitiveness and one-upmanship, but socially induced sex-role stereotyping as well. There are mysterious, personal dynamics which operate between lovers, more complicated than the degrees of acquaintanceship and friendship operating between male colleagues. There are expectations of how the lover fits roles in compulsive scenarios of sexual fulfilment in which she (more occasionally he) has been cast. And there are the expectations and fears raised by the prospect of long-term 'primary' relationships, and the demanding and mysterious spectres raised by the term 'love'. Mamet has said of *The Woods* that it is 'about heterosexual love. Why don't men and women get along? It's about the yearning to commit

yourself, to become less deracinated – or more racinated.'[1]
Arguably, the same theme is central to *Sexual Perversity in
Chicago*, though less obviously so. In both plays, attraction
develops between a relatively inexperienced pair, and both
plays reveal the complications of a situation where sexual
coupling has the potential to develop into the communion
of genuine love.

The differences in the plays' styles mostly result from
differences in focus and milieu. In *Sexual Perversity in
Chicago*, the 'episodic' structure with its thirty-four brief
scenes depicts the city milieu against which the affair is set,
and the forces which distract the lovers from their own
better impulses and condition them against each other. In
The Woods, the reduction in scope to just the two lovers
interacting in a rural environment, in three unbroken
scenes, is a dramaturgical equivalent of the characters' own
feelings of being anchored in time and space – and this
very stasis is a threat to their ability to be really intimate
with each other. In each play, Mamet uses different devices
and techniques to present his lovers' interactions, even
though there are some interesting parallels in their
discoveries and difficulties. And the tone is different. In
Sexual Perversity in Chicago, outrageous comedy is to the
fore, often caused by the ridiculous posturings of the
mentors and their bizarre sexual stories or fantasies. In *The
Woods*, the tone is for the most part lyrical and ruminative.

The plays have had very different production histories.
Sexual Perversity in Chicago is the play that first made
Mamet's name in Chicago and New York, and was his first
popular 'success'. Thematically, it deals almost as much
with male bonding as with heterosexual love, and can be
easily related to the other Chicago plays, especially since
the dialogue has a strong colloquial base. *The Woods*, on
the other hand, has been Mamet's most controversial play.

Several critics, including Bigsby, Cohn and Storey, have admired it. On the other hand, only the original St Nicholas production was fairly well received by reviewers. Both the New York productions – the first in 1979, directed by Grosbard, and the second in 1982, directed by Mamet – were panned. Some reviewers found the play moving and archetypal; others found it bogged down in commonplace realism. Some saw prophetic force manifested in the simple, repetitive words and phrases; others saw only banality. The play was hailed both as a tortured and personal male confessional and as a deeply misogynist play masquerading as a feminist one.[2]

In *Sexual Perversity in Chicago*, the plot develops from the kernel of two unisexual bondings. Danny Shapiro, an 'urban male in his late twenties', is impressed with an older 'friend and associate', Bernie Litko, who works in the same Loop office. Deb, a commercial artist, rooms with Joan, an *Angst*-ridden kindergarten teacher. Danny and Deb meet, are attracted, go to bed, and try to find a way to connect more deeply. The affair flowers briefly. They move in together; but they fight over trivialities, part once more, and take emotional refuge with their mentors. What saves this 'plot' from being familiar soap opera is that there is no clear causality for the failure. Again, a perverse dialectic is in operation. Through carefully controlled structural organisation, dialogue and character interaction, Mamet implies that a whole complex of forces – both within Dan and Deb, and without – negates whatever ability they have to open up to each other, even though they desperately want to.

The phalanx of inhibiting influences on the lovers is conveyed by the montage pattern of the thirty-four scenes. Their general length and patterning, some with as few as five lines, suggest the debilitating effects of day-to-day urban routine. This is also dramatised in the relatively trivial occasions – the fate of a television set, the absence of shampoo and clean panty-hose – for the lovers' tempers to flare up. Of course, the 'episodic' pattern is a scenic as well as a structural strategy, and suggests the dislocation and disjunction of experience in this urban milieu. No two successive scenes take place in the same location, and so the settings are necessarily spare and minimal – and in Takazauckas' production this very spareness made it possible for one scene to succeed another with the utmost speed. The montage thus underlines the environmental absence of significant, definitional objects to give the characters and audience the reassurance of place. Moreover, several short scenes show the characters delivering harangues to a 'captive audience' – buddies, co-workers, school pupils – whom we don't see. Both devices reinforce the impression that the characters are swept up in the urban environment and yet paradoxically divorced from it. Mamet implies that in the scenes in question it doesn't much matter where the characters are precisely, or whom they're talking to. Their attitudes are a rigid armoury, and they are locked in a frozen and societally conditioned relationship with their listeners, whose reactions are irrelevant. Near the end, there is a single scene where Deb is genuinely alone. She ponders the effect of substitution: how attachment to things might be a compensation for a failure of attachment to people. The genuine isolation here – there is no 'unseen' audience to whom Deb is speaking – is telling.

Crucial is the placing of many of the scenes suggesting the influence of the mentors Bernie and Joan. The two longest scenes, at the beginning and end of the play, involve the two men. These are scenes of ritual interaction, and they both underline the strength of the male bonding in a comic way, suggesting a prelude–coda model. In the first scene, Dan is Bernie's comic stooge, the feed for a pick-up fantasy which becomes increasingly improbable and sado-masochistic as it goes along; in the last, Dan is Bernie's peer as they sexually classify and ogle attractive women at a beach. More pertinent for the structure, however, are two pairs of successive scenes showing the debilitating effects of the mentors' own sexual anxieties on Dan and Deb. In Marshall Fields toy-store, Bernie reveals homophobic insecurities as well as his obsession with sado-masochistic sex as he inveighs against a 'fruit' at a games counter and tells Dan of a childhood assault by a 'dirty old man' at a cinema. And, in the following scene, Joan confides matter-of-factly to Deb about a sexual partner who prematurely ejaculated, and what she did about it – a typical and funny instance of Joan subjecting all sexual impulses to intellectual filtering. Two other tellingly juxtaposed scenes reveal the way the mentors react to the emotional confidences placed in them. In the first, Bernie ridicules to an unseen group of office buddies Dan's feelings about being in love. In the next, Joan lunches with Deb and tots up the odds against the affair lasting. And then there is the instance of a totally non-productive encounter of the mentors in a singles bar, followed, after a brief ironic scene, by the promising meeting of Dan and Deb in a library. Throughout, the scenes involving the mentor with a protégé are succeeded or interspersed with scenes in which the lovers are seen with each other, and this structure of comparisons is enhanced all along by differences in the kinds of language used. The effect of structure here is closely bound up with the 'effectiveness' of language.

The language is again significant as an index of the 'self-awareness' of the characters. It is most fluent and confident where they are at their flattest – those scenes in which the young people are being conditioned by their mentors. Each character here has a glib, 'received' kind of language to function with in social situations. The protégés have the less well-defined verbal profile. Dan's tends to be determined by a childish, ironic humour, while Deb's is marked by defensive catchphrases; but they also have traces of their mentors' verbal repertoire. Bernie's is a mixture of hip macho phrases, sado-masochistic porn shorthand, and rhythmic repetitions forming what Bigsby has called a 'reductive litany' to make women objects and thus remove their threat to him.[3] In the scene with Dan, the syncopations, the rhythm and the terms of reference are picked up and passed on. Equally sure but different in rhythm is the kind of dialogue which Joan shares with Deb. This is a kind of declamatory pop cynicism, punctuated with portentous silences which may have a modicum of genuine anxiety.

But the sterility and borrowed speciousness of this kind of patter is confirmed by the quality of the relationships of the two bonded pairs. In the case of the men, the relationship is sterile – not a genuine mentor–protégé relationship, because the mentor can impart no genuine insights about how to relate to women as distinct from 'scoring' off them, and, even at that level, the advice is spurious; and not friendship, since there is no mutual self-disclosure. In the case of the women, Joan can reveal no effective sympathy with Deb's attempts at optimism, and puts down as often as possible her need for encouragement. But the most devastating exposure of the masks of the mentors, which Richard Eder aptly called those of 'sexual conquest' and 'sexual put-down',[4] comes in their one scene together. Bernie and Joan encounter each other at a singles bar. To Bernie's assured but hackneyed come-on – in which he casts himself as a TWA meteorologist spending much time with charts – Joan ripostes by telling him that he does not interest her sexually. He persists. She gets up to leave, whereupon he plays his last card and calls her a 'cockteaser'. This she finds both insulting and sexually arousing – even as she complains in high dudgeon, she sits back down. But Bernie does not press his advantage – because his initial interest in Joan has been displaced by his need decisively to best her in a game of one-upmanship. Her sitting back down indicates that sex, at least, is a possibility. He doesn't want it. Instead, he calls for his check and leaves. The scene is one of Mamet's most mordantly hilarious. In its dialectical movement – its cross-over between a man who wants a woman and then doesn't, and a woman who doesn't want a man and then does – it parallels in miniature the development and demise of the central relationship between Dan and Deb.

The heart of the play is in the six scenes which Dan and Deb share alone. What becomes apparent in these scenes is that, though they can set aside their verbal armoury developed for social role-playing, they have nothing with which to replace it. The challenge here is to find ways to commune with each other beyond sex. Richard Eder remarked appositely of their first scene – in bed after sex – that it seems more difficult for Dan to invite Deb to go to dinner than it has been for him to make love to her. 'It is as if going to bed were the prelude and conversation the critical act.'[5] The talk here is comically banal, repetitive, gawkily austere; but there is also the subtext of sexual elation. It is a foretaste of the lovers' language in *The Woods*.

It turns out that their next scene determines the rest of their relationship. Some archly self-conscious bedroom chit-chat, in which sex organs and their functions are equated with TV commercials, slides into a declaration of love from Dan:

> DANNY. I love making love with you.
> DEBORAH. I love making love with you. (*Pause.*)
> DANNY. I love you.
> DEBORAH. Does it frighten you to say that?
> DANNY. Yes.
> DEBORAH. It's only words. I don't think you should be frightened by words.

Deb apparently reads Dan's confession that he is frightened as a sign that his declaration cannot be taken as a commitment; and so she lets them both off the hook by her remark that it's 'only words', implying that it's not authentic. But the basic distrust that Deb has of words is very revealing. For her, most words in most situations are apparently some sort of mask, an armour. She cannot believe that Dan's words here can be the expression of genuine feeling. So this is the turning-point in the relationship. Dan has lurched into a commitment. But Deb decertifies it, and Dan does not contradict her. And the scene ends.

Their next shared scene shows a deterioration as an argument flares up over a trivial cause, and the following one confirms the fact that they have crossed past one another, each reaching out to the other at the wrong time. Indeed, it is implied that they might be doing this deliberately, as part of a power-game of who needs whom most at any given time. Again they are in bed. Deb is asleep – or pretends to be. Dan tenderly tries to get her to talk to him, but fails. Whatever the reason for Deb's silence, the scene reinforces the fact that a two-way communion

between them is no longer possible. Shortly after this, Dan
resumes his visits to porno movie houses with Bernie.

All that is now left between the lovers is two short scenes
of argumentative abuse, the language confident and glib
once more as they ironically pick up each other's 'received'
language in combat, as well as refurbish their standard
armoury of catchphrases (Deb) and ironic humour (Dan).
Power-games within the relationship now dominate. At
one point, Dan tries for a reconciliation, asks her to come
over to him, and she replies, 'No. You come here for
christ's fucking sake. You want comfort, come get comfort.
What am I, your toaster?' Dan is not able to resurrect the
simple 'I love you' he made earlier, even though what he
soon says about Deb indicates she now wants him to:
'Everything's fine. Sex, talk, life, everything. Until you
want to get "closer", to get "better". Do you know what
the fuck you want? Push. You push me.' And then Deb
makes a charge that qualifies her earlier statement that
words cannot be trusted for she complains that he can never
express feelings other than through four-letter words or
groping inarticulateness: 'What are you *feeling*. Tell me
what you're *feeling*. Jerk.' Of course, the irony is that, in
the crucial bedroom scene, in which they almost
connected, he did tell her what he was feeling, and she
chose not to believe him.

In *The Woods*, the lovers' relationship is not merely the
centre of the play, but the whole of it – it is explored with
more fullness and complexity, and the tonality of the play is
totally different. Again, one of the lovers makes a
declaration that the other rejects. This time, it is the
woman who makes it. It is not spontaneous, but is
considered beforehand, and accompanied by the gift of an
inscribed bracelet. And again the partner who rejects the
initial declaration later feels the necessity to have it

reaffirmed when it is no longer possible. The pressure of unbroken time and space on the lovers, a condition which is almost a threatening challenge to achieve 'meaningful' intimacy, is built into the play's formal shape: three scenes which evoke the old-fashioned three-act play, titled 'Dusk', 'Night' and 'Morning'. The summer-home porch set suggests intersection between the spheres of the natural world and human domesticity; it also suggests openness, vulnerability, lack of protection. It is Labor Day weekend – the first weekend of autumn.

The number of traditional dramatic events in the play is slight, their ordering familiar. The lovers Ruth and Nick have come to the summer home, owned by his family, for the weekend. In Scene 1, they respond to the natural surroundings in their own way and prepare to make love. In Scene 2, in the middle of the night, he is disturbed, and she fails to comfort him. He abruptly wants sex, and she cannot respond. She gives him her gift, and he rejects it. They quarrel, and she decides to leave the next day. In Scene 3, the quarrel becomes violent – he knocks her off the porch into the mud. Contrite, he pours out his insecurities, makes a declaration of love, and begs her to stay with him. She comforts him with a story about the babes in the woods she had begun earlier, and the play ends in mid-sentence.

Once again, what is significant is not the few 'external' incidents, but the underlying pattern of the lovers' responses to each other, expressed in words and silences, which orchestrate the events in a very individual way. The lovers make disguised overtures to one another to enter into their scenarios of how life should be; their initial attempts to connect give way to power-plays in coercion and domination; and then there is a final breakthrough, for better or worse, to an area beyond the merely 'transactional', where masks are down. More so than in

Sexual Perversity in Chicago, the dialogue is the barometer of this pattern. It is highly formal and strict in its rhythms. It makes much use of repetition, and some of it seems trivial and inconsequential, so there is tension at times between the portentous rhythm of what is being said and the tenuousness of the actual content. These characteristics underline from the start the lovers' nervousness, their lack of security in the absence of the distractions and social masks easily assumed in the city, their nervousness in the face of what each might expect or demand of the other.

The pattern of the lovers' relationship is especially connected to two devices of dialogue. One is that of statement and reaction to the natural phenomena that surround them. The other is a mutual disclosure through storytelling, which Ruth seizes on as a means by which she and Nick can come to more intimacy.

The first is heavily concentrated in Scene 1, and dominated by the reactions of the reticent character – a problematic kind of scene frequently found in Mamet's work. This character is looking for something in the more loquacious one – 'Tell me', Nick twice urges Ruth, and also 'Say it again', and Ruth becomes more nervously talkative, possibly through a rising feeling of inadequacy in not saying what is needed. Finally, she turns Nick's demand back on him, urging him four times, 'Tell me.' The differences of their responses to nature – Ruth desperately outgoing and Nick cannily testing – illustrate that they are not 'in synch' and the scene becomes one of challenge and riposte. At the start, Ruth introduces an image of isolation: how a gull rushes to be in the sky alone and will not tolerate the presence of a companion. Intentionally or not, she is already throwing out the first challenge: in order to be closer they have to overcome the individual's urge to isolation. His response is a conventional connection-by-association to other birds – herons. The pattern intensifies. Ruth draws Nick's attention to some natural phenomenon, and her enthusiasm for crickets, frogs, fish and raccoons is repeatedly deflated by his responses. These are pragmatic corrections of her assumptions, or some irony that pulls them down to earth. Ruth's reactions to nature already characterise her as a kind of Earth Mother – she professes being alive to the natural cycle, and stresses how healthy things spring from the ground and finally return to it. Nick, on the other hand, is familiar with the surroundings from previous visits. He feels some wonder at how time has changed them, but not at the surroundings themselves. The rising lack of congruence between Nick and Ruth is especially signalled in two small incidents. When she talks of a raccoon, he says that they 'get in the garbage' and are vicious when caught and caged. It is as if he associates the caged raccoon with his own fear of entrapment. Shortly afterwards, as if contrite, he tries to share her enthusiasm for the natural surroundings by telling her he sees a beaver. This time, she pulls him to earth by insisting that all he sees is a floating log. They compromise by deciding that they are not looking at the same thing. The lack of congruence between their responses is temporarily dismissed by their imminent lovemaking at the end of Scene 1. But in Scene 2 the pattern resumes. Ruth, for example, wants to go for a walk in the rain; Nick does not. Ruth likes the feeling of rain on her face; Nick does not want to sit in an exposed area of the porch.

Bigsby has rightly stated that storytelling is fundamental in Mamet's work – the characters often use it as a tactic to create coherence in a world that for them lacks shape and meaning, or as an act of evasion, resistance, coercion or self-justification.[6] Occasionally, though, the stories are not tactical, but spontaneous exposures of vulnerability, an offering of self; and such moments open up the possibility of real contact. At first in *The Woods* the stories are tactical, though the lovers hardly seem to realise it. It is Nick who first mentions that his father would sometimes tell them stories, and a little later Ruth defines the way that she sees storytelling in their relationship: 'This is the best thing two people can do. / To live through things together. If they share what they have done before.' The stories they share, however, have to do not with their own experiences, but with Nick's father's and Ruth's grandmother's. Both include death, violence, and details which threaten the hearer. Moreover, they are coercive; they tend to cast the hearer in a role allied to one in the story.

The first story that Ruth tells is that of the babes in the woods, from the brothers Grimm. It has an unhappy ending, which she skips over; this story recurs, significantly, at the end of the play. Her real story, however, concerns the lady who first told this story to her – her grandmother; 'She was like the Earth. / She knew so many things.' Her husband was a man 'like Iron', with 'singed forearms'. They would lie all day in bed making love, saying nothing. The husband died a violent death at the hands of another, and all the clocks in the house stopped. Ruth's almost preternatural tale of passion is a threat, a challenge to Nick to respond psychically and sexually to Ruth with the same intensity. Moreover, the grandmother's necklace – which Ruth had lost, dropped into deep water because she was wearing it the wrong way – is reincarnated in Ruth's gift to Nick. He seems to regard it as a symbol of threatening entrapment and of the kind of sexuality and love that he might not be able to match.

Nick's story is equally threatening to Ruth. It concerns his father and another man, who fell into an abandoned Black Forest mine during the Second World War. Though they were rescued, the father's companion later beat his wife, developed a delusion that he had been kidnapped by Martians, went insane, and killed himself. He had been to the summer home as a guest during his final period of mental breakdown. Ruth later bitterly castigates the veiled threat in the story, with its motifs of misogyny and male bonding. The story's outcome reinforces her fear of isolation, indicated in the opening image of a solitary gull. At the end of Scene 2, she adds her own anecdote to the story – of Martians taking over the bodies of human beings, of their infiltrating marriages and becoming a husband or wife without the other partner knowing.

Both devices coalesce in the image of a wild bear, which becomes central in the culminating story of a nightmare told by Nick in Scene 3. In this image, too, is enshrined his conviction that he has no personalised speech with which to reveal and offer himself. So the image is tightly bound up with the play's impact and significance.

Ruth introduces the bear in Scene 1 as apparently just another image of nature. She tells Nick that, while she was on a walk the previous evening, a neighbour told her that they had built a house upon its cave, and it had come back 'when it was going to die'. Since the bear died, the image seems unthreatening, but Nick needs immediate reassurance. The event must have happened long ago, he insists. Moreover, such bears are found only in Canada, 'not around here'. In Scene 3, the bear becomes the major image in the first really personal story that Nick is able to tell Ruth – and this story is hardly tactical any longer, rather a desperate outlay of pain and insecurity. In the nightmare which Nick tells, the bear has appeared upright outside the house with a 'huge erection', waiting to reclaim the cave beneath the human structure, which is disintegrating in flames. Though Nick is sure that the bear can speak a human language, his thoughts are trapped inside his mouth. He 'CANNOT SPEAK. / If only he could *speak*. / If only he could say the thing he wants.' Ruth challenges this:

> RUTH. What does he want?
> NICK. I DO NOT KNOW!
> RUTH. No! (*She hits him.*)
>   *Pause.*
> NICK. It smells like fish up here.
>   *She hits him again.*
> RUTH. You speak to me.
> NICK. You know I cannot speak.

The bear is associated both with Nick's inability to verbalise his own feelings and with threat from a more powerful male who inhibits his self-assurance and self-realisation. Like the grandmother's husband, who was also associated with fire and singeing, the bear incorporates an image of masculinity that Nick feels threatened by and would like to embody. And the image also incorporates inarticulateness, a lack of a genuine felt language that might create contact. Ruth's violent reaction is both a rejection of the threatening bear image itself and of the idea that such a language cannot exist. The intensity of her reaction posits more hope for such a language developing between them than was possible for the lovers in *Sexual Perversity in Chicago*.

Nick's self-disclosure, then, has led to Ruth's angry rejection of some of the attitudes disclosed. When she wants to go swimming and be alone, he pours out a lacerating sense of despair and helplessness, which culminates with a declaration of love. Ruth had earlier hoped for this; but now it is finally offered in a context which prevents it from having any effect. It is a last-ditch plea for understanding and sympathy rather than an authentic commitment or an admission of moral responsibility. It is a plea for her to enter into his world, to accept him as he is, to accept his inarticulateness and his insecurities. Her flat 'Thank you' in response surely indicates that she realises this. She accepts for the time being the role of Earth Mother once again as she resumes the story of the babes in the woods, and the play ends on the phrase 'the next day', with its promises of continuation and the future, as the lights fade.

The Woods, along with several of Mamet's more recent plays, is a little self-conscious in its concern with representative allegory after the injunctions of Bettelheim and Campbell. Ruth and Nick are deliberately not fully 'characterised'. Certain facts about the characters' pasts are withheld, such as their jobs, how they first met, and the immediate circumstances which brought them to the summer home this particular weekend. This kind of detail is not relevant to Mamet's objectives here. The dialogue, with its spareness and formality, accords with this carefully limited perspective. There are differences here from *Sexual Perversity in Chicago*. There, the dialogue is ebullient and idiomatic, but it is socially conditioned dialogue for the most part. Though the characters in that play are not 'fleshed out' either, it is for the different reason that they are constricted because of their social masks and unwilling to expose aspects of self underneath.

Both these plays – and some in which lovers' relationships are less central – suggest a number of ancillary reasons for the failure of a man and woman to 'get along' and convert sexual attraction and gratification into something more transcendent. One is the rather shopworn association of sexual fulfilment with puritanical guilt. In *Sexual Perversity in Chicago*, it is illustrated comically and graphically in the monologue where Joan catches two (invisible) toddlers 'playing doctor'. She tells them that it is 'perfectly . . . natural', but that nevertheless they must wash their hands and their parents will be informed. In *The Woods*, after Nick has savagely knocked Ruth into the mud, she conjoins guilt with her recollection of the first time they made love: 'Blood. Your tongue. (*Pause.*) When I had you in me the first time. (*Pause.*) When you had me. (*Pause.*) Must I be *punished*? (*She starts to cry.*)'

The guilt associated with unlawful sexual gratification sentimentally determines the entire action of James M. Cain's *The Postman Always Rings Twice* (1934), which Mamet adapted as his first screenplay in 1979. Apart from a shift to third-person from first-person narrative, changes to the story were minimal. The heroine, Cora, a siren unhappy as the wife of a Greek restaurateur, persuades a Depression drifter, Frank, to murder her husband. Their sexual passion is first consummated not in an upstairs bedroom, as in Cain, but on a kitchen table with bread and dough roughly swept to the floor. Thereafter the lovers suffer an agony of mutual distrust and guilt. But just after their marriage, when Cora is pregnant and happiness seems within their grasp, she is killed in a car accident for which Frank is responsible. In the film (but not in the novella) this is because Frank becomes sexually distracted in a long embrace and does not keep his eyes on the road. In both media, a cautionary tale is told: untrammelled and adulterous sexual gratification leads to even worse crime, and crime does not pay.

Mamet implies that another difficulty facing lovers is that they will not recognise the 'hag' in each other. This image is introduced explicitly in *Sexual Perversity in Chicago* through a story which Joan recites to her pre-schoolers. It concerns a prince who comes home and finds that his beautiful wife has become a hag by night. She tells him that she can be beautiful during the daylight hours, to be admired, or beautiful at night, so that she can be enjoyed 'by the fireside, and so on. But for one half of the day I must be this old Hag you see before you.' The challenge is for lovers to accept the ugly, ego-ridden side of the partner; or perhaps the small irritants in the other's personality that they must learn to live with. Ruth says in *The Woods*, 'The worst part, maybe, is just learning little *things*. The *things* about each other. Other people.' Dan and Deb fail to make the transition from sex to something more like love because they cannot accept the 'hag' in each other. Ruth and Nick do so with more success, but it is not certain that the relationship can continue from that basis of total disclosure. The motif of the 'hag' – in reversed form, with the hero this time turning into a frog until he learns to put his ego aside – is central in one of Mamet's 'children's' plays, *The Frog Prince* (1982).

The plays underline the idea that most sex excludes the kind of genuine consonance that might lead to love – the partner is cast as sex object and thus becomes a two-dimensional puppet to gratify a one-sided fantasy. In *All Men are Whores: An Inquiry* (1977), Mamet suggests that sex should not be a 'consummation of predestined and unregenerate desire but rather . . . a two-part affirmation of our need for solace *in extremis*'.[7] In this play, three actors are transformed into different characters who deliver seventeen different monologues to the audience. The first and last are authorial inquiries about the difficulties that sex entails, and the intervening fifteen have the characters describing sexual or romantic encounters. None of them is happy. One partner does not fit the prescribed role in another's scenario; one is not able to commit himself to a deeper experience at the same time as the other; or the partners do not want the same kind of sexual experience. One of the episodes significantly carries over from *The Woods* the motif of a valuable gift from one partner to the other, which is wrongly received. Mamet drives home the idea that sex should be divested of power-games, one-sided expectations and fantasies, and reductive scenarios. Only then can it be a vehicle for consonance and communion.

And, yet, *Sexual Perversity in Chicago* and *The Woods* convey a sense that both affairs have had some value, have taught the lovers something about themselves, even if the results are painful. When Deb moves back in with Joan, she is clearly resentful of Joan's 'I told you so' platitudes. And Dan's parting shot at a passing beach girl who ignores him – 'Deaf *bitch*' – can easily suggest that he regrets what he has lost.

5
Learning

The largest group of Mamet plays presents a picture of
protagonists less circumscribed by social conditioning.
They fight with more success to break through social masks
and constraints and to move towards communion with each
other. Again, the dialogue is an indication of their degree
of co-option by social influences. When it breaks down and
loses its colloquial assurance, when it becomes groping,
repetitive and spare, or when it sputters, collapses and
restarts, there is an indication that the characters are
vulnerable and uncertain. They are possibly shedding their
social roles, trying to find an alternative way of being – and
ultimately communicating. But at all times the movement
of characters along this path is threatened by forces both
without and within them – the same kind of social and
sexual pressures as operate more forcefully in the plays
already examined.

In the plays considered here the relationship is an
educative one between two males, often taking the form of
mentor–protégé. It is more positive than the sterile, usually

competitive, bonding of, say, Bernie and Dan in *Sexual Perversity in Chicago*, or the gentle but ineffective bond of Don and Bob in *American Buffalo*. One of its distinguishing features is that what is taught has authenticity – based on genuine experience or skill. Mamet has spoken of his belief that this kind of bonding can be efficacious. For example, at the fiftieth anniversary of the Neighborhood Playhouse, he stated that theatre skills 'cannot be communicated intellectually. They must be learned first-hand in long practice under the tutelage of someone who learned them first-hand.'[1] By extension, the same principles could be applied to other professions, trades, arts. Such educative relationships – of the kind shown in *Squirrels*, *A Life in the Theatre* and *Lakeboat* – are different from the 'partnerships' sought in *American Buffalo* and *Glengarry Glen Ross*. The men acknowledge that they are not equal in professional knowledge, experience or expertise; and that is a safeguard against peer rivalry. Consequently, mutual support and learning have a chance to win out against urges toward competition. Tensions can develop: the mentor may be jealous when the protégé develops in a way that surpasses him, or progresses against his values or expectations. Or the protégé may find, on his part, that familiarity breeds contempt. Sometimes, as in *Lakeboat*, the professional specifications of the bond are not important; in that case the transference theme – of the challenges and responsibilities passed from a retiring to an emergent generation – becomes more prominent. *The Duck Variations* is a special case; there the relationship is more one of teacher–pupil in two old men who are much the same age.

All that 'happens' in *The Duck Variations* is that two old men sit on the park bench near a lake and build an encounter from what they see and choose to talk about.

They are old 'friends', so this is a social ritual. The title
indicates the unpromising main topic – but ducks prove a
trampoline for observations about such things as the
poisoning of the environment, the endurance of
generational cycles and the inevitability of death. This last
is a topic they cannot face together until the end of the play.

Various formal elements are strongly foregrounded.
Early as it is, the play reveals Mamet's own voice and
signature, but it is also the play in which influences from
Beckett and Pinter are most obvious, as several critics have
noted. The very stasis of the action, the fact that these two
old friends are partly making conversation to fend off
facing a void which may terrify them, is redolent of *Waiting
for Godot*; and there is a good deal of comedy that accrues,
as in Pinter, from the 'gap between the mundane nature of
the subject-matter and the elevated language that the
characters apply to it'.[2] *The Duck Variations* might be
called one of Mamet's Apollonian plays, and it grew from a
strongly formal purpose and inspiration. It was influenced
by a preoccupation at the time with dialogue as music, and
by Aaron Copland's book *What to Listen for in Music*.[3] The
structure comprises fourteen 'variations', prefaced by the
direction that there should be brief intervals between them
*'analogous to the space between movements in a musical
presentation'*.[4]

At the same time, however, George Aronovitz and Emil
Varěc are not just archetypes – they are solidly grounded in
verisimilitude. Their dialogue may be cast by a musical
shaping-principle, but it 'derives from listening to a lot of
old Jewish men all my life, particularly my grandfather'.[5]
The idiomatically grounded dialogue places the lake they
watch as somewhere near Chicago, not in Beckett country.
And their encounter on the park bench is not just a
controversational strategy to distract them from realities

they cannot face, but the playing-out of a dynamic human relationship between two personalities of quite different temperament and cast of mind who nevertheless need each other. Mamet presents a relationship which, while it cannot be classified as mentor–protégé (because the men are much of an age) or a 'partnership' (because it is not grounded in 'business' co-operation) is strongly influenced by the characteristics of both.

George is the dominant personality. But he is prone to discursive ruminations, to extrapolate generalities from questionable premises. Some of these are seductively exciting, especially when they involve flights of imaginative fantasy and storytelling. Emil has a more logical mind, which works through careful accretion of evidence, and through cause-and-effect. Mental leaps scare him. He is more sentimental than George, however, and he shores up his life against unpleasant realities with comforting platitudes and maxims that he doesn't want bowled over. When they are, he is often fascinated and frightened. When George cuts too close to the grain by comparing ducks' life-cycles to humans', he remarks, 'You know, it is a good thing to be perceptive, but you shouldn't let it get in the way.' When George challenges his cliché that 'Nothing that lives can live alone' by citing the case of the cactus, he protests, 'I don't want to hear it. If it's false don't waste my time and if it is true I don't want to know.'

Each character, then, has a social role that shores him up against silence and too much self-questioning. While this restricts the depth of the friendship, it gives it a dynamic quality. George is the chief 'storyteller' and authority, and Emil is usually the eager learner, anxious both to receive George's teaching and to challenge it when necessary. The major challenge comes in Variation 11, which marks the greatest disagreement between the two, ostensibly over whether spectator sports are responsible for the balance of nature. At the variation's beginning, Emil apologises to George for having hurt his feelings, apparently because he feels that earlier he was challenging George too vehemently. But the real cause of the fight surely relates to Emil's sudden need to take the lead here, to be the authority. The challenge collapses, both because of George's will to assert himself, and because, no matter how much Emil might protest at George's lack of logic, both know that Emil is mesmerised by the vistas that only George can reveal. Emil is chastened and apologises.

Because the social roles of George and Emil are so stable, the dialogue moves with fluidity and sure, effective rhythms; there are few hesitations, collapses and dysfunctions. The rhythms are deceptively ruminative on the printed page, but can come across in performance as a dynamic series of questions and answers, George's answers sometimes challenged or compounded by another eager question. The most typical pattern of interaction is one of Emil hanging anxiously on the edge of George's scenarios, repeatedly punctuating them with an anxious 'Yes' or 'Yeah' or imperious 'Tell me' – but with George retaining control as 'teacher'. The following example is from Variation 5:

> GEORGE. . . . The Stratosphere, particularly the lower stratosphere, is becoming messy with gook.
> EMIL. Eh?
> GEORGE. According to the weatherman.
> EMIL. *Our* Stratosphere?
> GEORGE. Everybody's. Because it's all the same thing.
> EMIL. Eh?
> GEORGE. As if you drop a pebble in a pond and the ripples spread you-know-not-where . . .

EMIL. Yes?

GEORGE. So, when you stick shit up in the Stratosphere . . .

EMIL. Yes?

GEORGE. You got the same problem.

EMIL. What kinds of gook?

GEORGE. All kinds. Dirt . . .

EMIL. Yes.

GEORGE. Gook . . .

EMIL. No good.

GEORGE. Automotive . . .

EMIL. Yeah.

GEORGE. Cigarette smoke. It's all up there. It's not going anywhere.

EMIL. Yeah.

GEORGE. They're finding out many things about the world we live in from the air.

EMIL. Yes.

GEORGE. For, in Many ways . . . the air is more a part of our world than we would like to admit. Think about it.

EMIL. I will.

The dialogue gains a sense of sureness, even at times a pontifical character, from the teacher–pupil relationship; and, as in *Squirrels* and *A Life in the Theatre*, the comedy comes when we perceive that what is taught is at times banal, out of proportion to the portentousness of the dialogue which clothes it.

The climax of the play, in Variation 13, repeats the essential pattern of the above passage. George has a vision of the duck's death in a hunt, and Emil hangs on to it. And here, for the first time, neither character shies away from a vision of death, a vision that earlier they were not ready to face at the same time.

In the final Variation (14), there is irony in Emil's reference to the way that old Greek men would watch birds in their dotage, 'Incapable of working. / Of no use to their society.' Neither man applies this to his condition. But this hardly qualifies the positive bent of most of the play. Steven H. Gale has remarked that 'ultimately the importance of their conversation lies not in occasional insights but in the fact that they are conversing'.[6] But they are more than conversing: they are carrying out action in Mamet's and Stanislavsky's sense, each exercising will to contact, then away, then back again, in a dynamic bond of friendship.

A more clearly defined mentor–protégé relationship provides the major focus in two other early Mamet plays, *Squirrels* and *A Life in the Theatre*.

Of all Mamet's full-length plays, *Squirrels* is the one in which the formal and metaphorical means of expression – the allegorical dimensions of the action – most outweigh a grounding in verisimilitude. The central characters are two writers, Art and Edmond, the latter the young employee of the former as well as a protégé. Art cannot finish a story about a squirrel in a park who bites the hand of a man who feeds him. Work has reached a standstill because he is too bound up with the process of incident- and word-selection. A third character, the Cleaning Lady, pops in and out of Art's office. She was once Art's lover and shares the difficulty he experiences in completing stories. But Edmond soon finds a peer relationship with her in which he experiences some release from the frustrating apprenticeship to Art. There are many stylistic features of the action that could be labelled Absurdist – monologues delivered directly to the audience, foregrounding of theatrical references and conventions, a presentational use of certain props.

But the action involving the mentor–protégé relationship does have a clear-enough shape and crests to a climax in which the transfer of power between the generations does occur. At first, Edmond toadies to Art, suffering his clearly ineffectual attempts to continue the story. Then Edmond asks to 'try one', and, when he persists in this initiative, Art withdraws. First he does not listen to the suggestions, then he gets hungry and eats up Edmond's bag lunch, and finally he retreats to the toilet. Art then tries to mollify Edmond and fails, and so tries abuse as a last resort to keep him in line: 'just keep your mouth shut and shut up'. Finally, the subject-matter of the story is changed from squirrels to geese and Edmond seems to have more control. But, if this is a transfer of power from one generation to another, Edmond has picked up some of Art's worst faults, including tendencies to generalise grandiloquently and to become bogged down in constipating trivia. Nevertheless, he confides to the Cleaning Lady that he has learned something. For him, 'true employment of inspiration is in formal endeavors where the inspiration can take form. We *have* been working. It isn't as if we'd been idle.'

In *Squirrels*, even more than in Mamet's other plays, choice of words is the primary focus of the actions that the characters perform; for the bond between mentor and protégé is based on professional writing-skills. The choice of words as action is so prominent that it is difficult for a director to incorporate organic and relevant activity and 'business'. Because the mentor–protégé bond gives the characters role definition, the dialogue has a sureness about it, but there is also uncertain idiomatic allegiance. The reiterated motif of trivial, incomplete stories is funny at first, but outstays its welcome in a play of this length. One cautiously favourable review of the Chicago production conceded that, 'because it is a play so deeply and intimately connected with language, *Squirrels* needs unusually intense attention from its audience'.[7] But this kind of attention somewhat vitiates comic relaxation and enjoyment. We are led into a jungle of semantic hair-splitting over trivial content which pays fewer and fewer comic dividends.

The sense of strain that characterises *Squirrels* is completely absent from *A Life in the Theatre*, which reads and plays in a deceptively effortless manner. The movement to a climax of a transfer of power from mentor to protégé is the same, but it is rendered with more subtlety. The characters are this time not animated Absurdist metaphors, but well-observed individuals who at the same time carry representative weight. Apart from a silent stage-manager, who makes possible some costume sleight-of-hand so that the play can flow, Mamet concentrates on just two characters: Robert, an aging leading actor in a regional repertory company, and John, an eager newcomer. The structure is made up of a series of short scenes showing the working-relationship of Robert and John 'backstage', interspersed with scenes from the company's repertoire in which they appear 'on stage'. This formal design is elegant and firm, but not obtrusive. It is accented by having the backstage scenes played downstage, and the onstage scenes in front of a second curtain installed upstage and opened when appropriate. *'Thus we see the actors' backs during their onstage scenes, and a full view of them during the backstage scenes – in effect, a true view from backstage.'* Though the theatrical environment is minimally shown, the result is not skimpy allegory but poetic suggestiveness, for appropriate costumes and props help create the theatrical ambiance. This is especially effective in the onstage scenes, which are stylised into, at times, hilarious parody.

The foundations of the bonding between Robert and John are laid down in the long opening scene. The men barely know each other, but they feel mutual rapport because of a just-concluded successful opening night. There is a ritual exchange of compliments over each other's scenes, a qualification in the younger man's praise of the older which is soon deferentially retracted, a collusive disparagement of the charms and professional ability of a female colleague; a hesitant invitation to supper from John to Robert, which is eventually accepted; and a rough equivalent of thumb-slitting and blood-mixing when John wipes a bit of make-up from Robert's face with his own spittle.

At first John is like a puppy dog, actually bending down and knocking on wood when Robert requests it and grateful for the opportunity to lap up professional advice. But the honeymoon is soon over. Robert waspishly resents John's apparent personal involvement with someone outside the theatre – it seems that he has no equivalent relationship. And John begins to see that Robert's habit of grandiose generalising from dubious premises has an air of spurious pretension about it and at times a downright inconsistency. In the amusing *barré* scene where the men are exercising, Robert first insists that vocal beauty is much more important than physical for an actor – then finally reveals that after all he is obsessed with personal appearance. The first serious friction in the relationship comes when Robert criticises John for walking on his scene, and John perceives the motivation as essentially one of professional jealousy. But he gets his revenge by enjoying Robert's discomfiture at a broken fly; and helps him mend it, very imperfectly, before Robert goes onstage. Thereafter, rivalry begins to catch up with mentorship, and 'business' one-upmanship begins to rear its head, although the original terms of the relationship do continue. John still lights Robert's cigarette, and he still learns from him, though with his guard up. And much of what he learns is valuable. For instance, Robert tells John that as an actor he can never control what people think of him, just his actions and intentions onstage – a summary of what Mamet himself constantly reminds his acting-students. But John is not grateful for the advice – 'I think I know that.' The advice is again given in circumstances where it is tarred with professional jealousy.

A central dichotomy comes into focus in Scene 17, when John loses his temper at Robert's constant ritualising, and extrapolating grandiose generalities from mundane specifics. From this point on the play gains in power. The dichotomy has to do with the way that Robert and John view the nature of the theatre. Up to this point, Robert regards the theatre as mostly an analogue of life. Theatre provides him with a social role, and so an identity. He uses his place in this regional theatre as a comforting bulwark against both a larger professional marketplace, and the non-professional life outside. So for him the 'Theatre's a closed society' in which '*forms* evolve'. Robert explains further that 'One must speak of these things, John, or we will go the way of all society . . . Take too much for granted, fall away and die. (*Pause.*) On the boards, or in society at large. There must be law, there must be a reason, there must be tradition.' Built into this tradition is the omnipotence of the mentor; the older generation instructs the younger from the 'quality of its actions. Not from its discourse, John, no, but organically. (*Pause.*) You can learn a lot from keeping your mouth shut.' Once again, the very final statement is different in tone and rhythm from the preceding rhetoric, and undermines its validity. The whole credo points up Robert's rigidity and his self-protective need to ritualise relationships. By contrast, John assumes that the theatre is a part of life, though he seems to know that it involves special discipline and he is eager to learn from his more experienced colleague. But he has relationships outside the company, auditions for outside productions and has the ambition, and probably the talent, to take him beyond regional repertory.

It is in Scene 23 that the relationship between Robert and John reaches flashpoint. Mamet has said that 'in any really intense friendship, one looks for a precipitating event',[8] and so it proves here. Robert realises that theatre-as-closed-system is not enough for him – and with that realisation he lets his need for deeper human contact break through the mask of mentor. In a lengthy plea to John, he accepts the alternative to his earlier model – he now concedes that theatre and life are all one. Consequently, he comes close to telling John that he is like a son: 'I'm so *gratified* (if I may presume, and I recognize that it may be a presumption) to see you . . . to see the *young* of the Theatre . . . (And it's *not* unlike one's children) . . . following in the footpaths of . . . following in the footsteps of . . . those who have gone before'. As often in Mamet, the climactic lowering of social mask is signalled by changes in the dialogue. Earlier, Robert's speech is sprung with the certitude and confidence of an almost-iambic pattern, a spare and non-repetitive confidence of address. Clashes in different levels of language are smoothed over with assertive rhythms. But here Robert's rhetorical confidence drains away; he fumbles, pauses, repeats himself. The personal reaching-out, the confession of a personal need, involves not only the lowering of the mentor mask but, with it, the distance from which he maintains his authority. John's response – which is to simply to answer Robert's long speech and reiterated 'Goodnight' with a reiterated 'Goodnight' of his own – indicates that the charge of being

Robert's surrogate son may be a heavy load to bear. Perhaps a heavier one is what has been hinted at earlier in the play, that the sexuality of mentor and protégé differ. This might explain John's reluctance to open up in a more fully personal way to Robert. In any case, Mamet believes that there is an element of sexual ambiguity in any relationship that involves a mentor and a protégé.[9] But the scene does not end with these goodnights. John thinks he is alone in the theatre and continues to rehearse; Robert, still in the wings, surreptitiously watches. The mentor is checking the protégé, to see whether he will surpass him; the protégé, in an angry 'Shit' of protest, apparently realises that he will be foreever measuring himself in his mind against the mentor's judgement.

At the end of the play, the relationship continues in a kind of stalemate, the roles not entirely reversed or abandoned, the transfer of power from one generation to another not totally complete. However, Robert's career does decline perceptibly; no longer with his mentor mask in place as protection, he fishes for sympathy. He forgets his lines on stage and has the curtain rung down on him. He cuts his wrist, perhaps partly in another desperate ploy for John's sympathy and endorsement. But, at the end of the play, things are again on a more even keel. John makes a ritual gesture of obeisance to Robert when he asks for a $20 loan to go out with friends; but Robert has to be prodded, almost pleaded with, to reverse the ritual gesture of the play's beginning and light John's cigarette.

It is tempting to try to find traces of Absurdism in the play, similar to those of *Squirrels*, and of course they are present, but it is easy to push this too far. On the page, the play seems 'episodic', particularly because of the onstage scenes – but in fact discontinuities can be marginal in a production such as that directed by Gutierrez, which emphasised flow. After the final scene with John, Robert is left alone on the dark stage:

> ROBERT (*to himself*). The lights dim. Each to his own home. Goodnight. Goodnight. Goodnight.

Mamet's stage direction reveals that this is in no way a presentational address to the audience, and in performance it registers more as affectionate sentimentality than as Absurdist gesture. The significance of *A Life in the Theatre* cannot be netted by zipping it up in a Beckett–Stoppard bag: like Robert's fly, the zip tends to stick in the open position. Rather, the significance lies in the precise structuring and development of the central relationship between Robert and John.

Lakeboat, though in its original form Mamet's first performed play, was totally revised for its professional premiere by the Milwaukee Repertory Theatre ten years later. John Dillon, the artistic director, gave Mamet a 'whole bunch of wonderful suggestions' over several months, which involved not only cutting but also repositioning and restructuring the original material.[10] The play shows signs of its earlier origins in its greater amount of 'characterising' detail, but it wears this realism lightly, and there is no self-conscious allegorising. As in *A Life in the Theatre*, male bonding is a major theme, but it is seen here in more general terms. A young newcomer is initiated into the rites of a world he will not make permanently his, so his apprenticeship is temporary. But a mentor–protégé bond operates in a larger sense. A young man is accepted by his elders, and he in turn faces the responsibilities of adulthood at the same time as his older associates become aware that their best years have passed them by.

This time, the milieu is that of freshwater sailors on the

Great Lakes cargo freighters. The duration of the action is a voyage from East Chicago to Duluth. The newcomer is eighteen-year-old Dale Katzman, an English-literature sophomore back home in Chicago for the summer. He is a last-minute replacement for a missing night cook. As he is booked, Dale briefly (and for the only time) addresses the audience. This gesture is enough to stamp him as a privileged character – and an outsider. The steamer is carrying iron ore, he tells us, and is named *T. Harrison*, a home for forty-five men. We encounter seven more of them as the voyage progresses. The play ends with Dale's imminent departure as the boat is about to dock in Duluth; news is received that the missing crewman has caught the train north to rejoin it.

The sea voyage, of course, is a Romantic motif in American literature and drama. The first short plays of the young O'Neill reflected his seafaring adventures in exotic locales, though for the time the plays exemplified gritty realism. At first glance, the action of *Lakeboat* seems like a mordant comment on this tradition. The voyage is limited in scope, unromantic in nature, and, for most of the men on board, boringly routine. Moreover, the world of the Great Lakes steamers is obsolescent. The early years of the steamers were romantic indeed, and even as late as 1970 the trade was strong. But then it fell away, partly through competition with new, powerful ocean freighters. Ultimately, the lakeboat has mixed import as a symbol. 'Functional in design, graceless in appearance, the lakeboat inspires none of the romance that surrounds her salt-water cousins.' Yet 'in its graceless majesty it stands as a paean to the past, a working reminder of the roots of a country and a people in their prime'.[11] Again, the Mamet liking for dialectic is in operation, as the paean to the past collides with the trivia of the present.

1. Gregory Mosher's production of *American Buffalo* as presented at the St. Nicholas Theatre, 1975. From left: J. J. Johnson as Don, Mike Nussbaum as Teach, William H. Macy as Bob. Courtesy of the Chicago Public Library. Special Collections Division. Copyright: James C. Clark.

2. The 1979 revival of *A Life In the Theatre* at the Goodman Studio, directed by
Mosher. Cosmo White as John, left, and Mike Nussbaum as Robert. Courtesy
Goodman Theatre. Copyright: Diane Schmidt.

3. Rob Knepper as Dale, left, listens to Jack Wallace as Fred recounting his high-school conquest story in the Goodman *Lakeboat*, 1982. Courtesy Goodman Theatre. Copyright: Linda Schwartz.

4. *Edmond* at the Goodman Studio in 1982, directed by Mosher. The final scene between Colin Stinton as Edmond (bottom bunk) and Paul Butler as the Black Prisoner. Courtesy Goodman Theatre. Copyright: Linda Schwartz.

5. Gregory Mosher (left) and David Mamet at the first rehearsal of *Glengarry Glen Ross* at the Goodman Studio in January, 1984. Courtesy Goodman Theatre. Copyright: Dallas A. Saunders.

6. Robert Prosky as Levene, left, pleads with J. T. Walsh as Williamson in Act I Scene 1 of *Glengarry Glen Ross* in Mosher's production for the Goodman that later transferred to Broadway. Setting by Michael Merritt. Courtesy Goodman Theatre. Copyright: Brigitte Lacombe.

7. *Glengarry Glen Ross,* Act I Scene 2 of Mosher's production: Mike Nussbaum as Aaronow, left, and James Tolkan as Moss. Courtesy Goodman Theatre. Copyright: Brigitte Lacombe.

8. *Glengarry Glen Ross*, Act I Scene 3 of Mosher's production. William L Petersen as Lingk, left, and Joe Mantegna as Roma. Courtesy of Goodman Theatre. Copyright: Brigitte Lacombe.

9. *Glengarry Glen Ross*, Act II of Mosher's production. J. T. Walsh as Williamson, left, and Robert Prosky as Levene. Courtesy Goodman Theatre. Copyright: Brigitte Lacombe.

10. *Glengarry Glen Ross*. Act II of Mosher's production. Mike Nussbaum as Aaronow, left, and Joe Mantegna as Roma. Courtesy Goodman Theatre. Copyright: Brigitte Lacombe.

11. *The Water Engine* in its revival on the Goodman mainstage, directed by Steven Schachter. Centre: William H. Macy as Lang. Courtesy Goodman Theatre. Copyright: Kevin Horan.

12. *The Shawl* in Mosher's premiere for the New Theatre Company, Chicago, in 1985. The seance scene with Gary Cole as Charles, (left background), Lindsay Crouse as Miss A, and Mike Nussbaum as John. Courtesy Goodman Theatre. Copyright: Brigitte Lacombe.

The motifs of dirt, boredom, obsolescence, and a sense of wasted and unfulfilled lives are set against the compensatory possibilities of simple affection and support between men brought into teamwork largely through happenstance. The men have limited education; but, unlike the striving characters of the 'business'-dominated plays, they accept their lot, which they have perhaps chosen because it leaves them free to cut loose from marriages and domestic duties, booze all night, and not be too competitive. Of course, this does not make them constantly happy, and they themselves recognise that such 'freedom' is a chimera. But none of them say, like Aaronow in *Glengarry Glen Ross*, 'Oh, God, I hate this job.' Indeed, when Dale talks of the advantages of straight shifts, the older regular Joe says to him that 'it's like having a *job* for chrissakes', implying that most of the men live with the myth that they are not working at all. With this attitude, there is no threat. To some, introspection, revelation and wonder are possible. But at the same time, they test themselves in ludicrously competitive rituals and conflict over trifling routines such as fire-drill and sandwich-making, which become magnified in importance. They become devices to score points over each other, to stave off the boredom of the voyage itself. They sometimes quarrel over trivia – whether someone has really been to Italy or not, or whether a film hero is a 'stud' or a phony. Such rituals are reinforced by the largely formal, but pervasive, hierarchy on the boat: the firemen on the bottom, the stewards next, then the able-bodied seamen, on up to the second and first mate, who was once a skipper but somehow got demoted. The depth of the play, its sadness, are opened out of an unforced cause: it is natural that a newcomer in a stable, blue-collar world should draw out boasts, confessions and fantasies that men tend to withhold from more permanent team-mates. In their interactions when Dale is not present, the men reveal mutual concern and support, but their self-disclosure to each other is guarded and statistical. Dale acts as a catalyst, with somewhat different results, on the two men who are most aware that their lives on the lakeboats have denied them other options. But Dale does not remain only a catalyst. He gains confidence because of acceptance by these tougher, more seasoned men – hence undergoes a rite of passage.

The play is printed in twenty-eight titled scenes; but the set is a unit construction of the whole boat, so there is hardly any pause at all between each scene, and several scenes are continuous and run directly into each other. There is none of the dislocation of *Sexual Perversity in Chicago* or *Edmond*. The voyage itself, and Dale's arrival and replacement, give further formal cohesion. But the most important shaping principle of the action is Dale's rite of passage itself and his friendship with two of the seamen, Fred and Joe. The action accordingly falls into two stages.

At first, Dale's main interactions are with Fred, but they do not have the authentic give-and-take of nascent friendship. Fred wants to impress Dale, and is too locked into projecting a social role of macho stud to be capable of self-disclosure. The first scene they share is a little reminiscent of the opening Dan–Bernie scene in *Sexual Perversity in Chicago*. The younger man, all ears, is treated to a graphic description of a high-school sexual conquest, which, unlike Bernie's fire and flak-suit fantasy, is probably grounded in an actual event. But its moral is similar to Bernie's: 'THE WAY TO GET LAID IS TO TREAT THEM LIKE SHIT.' Later, we see that Fred's inability to be genuinely open is a problem for him. He soliloquises by the rail and is full of power fantasies he spins to himself as audience. When he does talk to his peers, he is guarded about his two marriages, both of which have been failures. On the other hand, he admires the fascistic sadism of the movie hero Jonnie Fast, and champions his aggressive macho qualities even in the teeth of ridicule. Perhaps most revealing is the fact that he admires the racetrack, and the principle it represents – all or nothing, win or lose. 'It's like life without all the complicating people.'

The next scene that Fred and Dale share (15) is awkward, and Mamet indicates this through dialogue. It sputters and sits uneasily in its rhythms because both men hold onto masks that do not really suit them. Fred talks of his first marriage and child; but he still wants to appear cool and limits self-disclosure. In order to compete, Dale talks tough, forces his rhythms, and peppers his syntax with forced blue-collar idiom. The Dale–Fred relationship, like that of Bernie and Dan in *Sexual Perversity in Chicago*, is hopelessly delimited by macho role-playing, and Fred has set the pace.

Dale finds more depth in his dealings with Joe, a sailor even more confused and misplaced than Fred – but not a man afraid of self-disclosure. Like Fred, he can tell stories, but without necessarily putting himself into a heroic or even favourable light. His stories are of the kind that Nick learns to tell, after painful struggle, in *The Woods*; or that Bernie is able to tell his daughter Carol in *Reunion*. Joe communes with Dale without patronising, so much so that Dale reacts honestly, without changing his attitudes to agree with him. Joe is of Polish ancestry, and in an earlier scene he tells Fred of the severe discipline he knew at home, a discipline founded on male authority, brutality and obedience. This partly explains his grudging acceptance of the rank hierarchy on the boat, which operates at times with patent absurdity and elicits more inconsistent reactions from him than from any of the others. Joe also has an ingrained gentility, which comes out in the respectful way he addresses Dale and the concern with which he draws him out. His friendship with Dale is gratuitous in the sense that no professional mentor–protégé relationship is involved. He senses that Dale is too far apart from him in education and aspiration ever to opt for the kind of work he has made his life, and that the boy has a bright future, whereas Joe has worked for twenty-three years on the lakeboats and has never even shipped salt. But a sense of two different lives coming together, able to communicate mutual concern, is strong in the three scenes these men share. The men share a sense that they are out of their element – one temporarily, and one permanently. They have been brought into contact through alienation from their surroundings.

The first scene, 'The Bridge', takes its title from an actual bridge under which the boat is passing. Joe makes some comments about the bridge's double function: it both has utilitarian value and is nice to look at. This in itself is a notable observation for Joe to make; the bridge is still wondrous to him. Elsewhere in the play, Mamet stresses that interest is in the eye of the beholder, not the scene. The first mate wonders why some shipboard visitors would find loading rocks in the hold interesting, and Skippy replies, 'It's all a matter of perspective.' But in this scene Joe is shedding an ironical, even cynical, role that he puts on for his regular team-mates. So here again the language becomes awkward as social masks are set aside. The scene never slips into sentimentality, for Joe reveals some envy of Dale's youth and advantages as well as concern for him. And Dale, in spite of his education, cannot find the words to give Joe the right support, to convince him that his life still has possibilities. The drive towards mutual contact is present less in the halting, reiterated words of the scene and their banal surface meaning than in the subtext – in the intent of the characters that the reiterations and the rhythms of the words uncover:

> JOE. You got your whole life ahead of you. I mean, you're not a *kid* or anything . . . you're a man. You're a young man. But you got it made.
>
> DALE. What are you talking about, Joe?
>
> JOE. Ah, you know what I'm saying.
>
> DALE. You're not an old man, Joe. What are you talking about?
>
> JOE. Ah, you know what I'm saying to you. I just wanted to tell you, Dale. I just wanted to let you know. So you'll understand. I mean. I've lived longer than you have. And at this stage one can see a lot of things in their proper light. And . . . you're a bright kid.

Again, as in *A Life in the Theatre*, a kind of generational transfer of power and responsibility is implicit here, and again the young man instinctively balks at the mandate.

In their next shared scene, Joe (very much like Robert in *A Life in the Theatre*) throws even stronger distress signals to the younger man, perhaps fishing for sympathy, or for a deeper avowal of concern. He hints at suicide, at serious illness. Dale does show concern, and tells him to see a doctor – but also tells him that it is probably not as serious as Joe imagines.

Their final beer-drinking scene cements the relationship and contrasts it to the one between Dale and Fred. Unlike Fred, Joe can reveal things that he has guarded, things that do not accord with a macho image – such as that, at the age of fifteen, he wanted to be a ballet dancer. Then he leads into a story that is the antithesis of Fred's high-school conquest – a pathetic, comic one in which he uncovers the futility and the onanistic basis of many male power fantasies. It begins with a false detail Fred would have let stand:

> JOE. I had this gun when I lived over on the South Side. I won it in a poker game.
> DALE. Yeah.
> JOE. Aaaaaaah, I fucking bought it off the bumboat in Duluth. Why lie? Forty bucks.

Joe recounts how, one night, he started playing a cops-and-robbers game with the gun in the mirror, how he put the barrel in his mouth and considered suicide, and how, finally, he tucked it under his pillow with one hand and masturbated with the other. Life may well be absurd and lonely for Joe, and ultimately for most of the men stuck on the lakeboats for their whole working lives. But Mamet suggests that a genuine effort can create circumstances in which some sort of sharing can take place. During this scene, there is no awkwardness or inarticulateness in Joe; the language flows.

In the final scene, Joe tells the others, including Dale, that the errant night cook is returning, and remarks, 'Well, I'll be glad to have him back.' Dale says nothing other than to offer him a coffee. The inevitability of his moving on is part of the rite of passage, part of the natural cycle of life – and easier than it would be for a professional such as John in *A Life in the Theatre*, where the arena of apprenticeship has been tighter, with a high stake. The casual ending to *Lakeboat* defuses sentimentality without invalidating the arc of contact that charges the play.

6
Communion

Learning is a major instrument in Mamet for communion between male characters; but there are also plays in which communion is seen as the result of a lonelier and more trial-ridden process. These plays comprise some of Mamet's earliest and more recent work, and some of them have been undervalued.

In *The Verdict*, *Edmond* and *Lone Canoe*, the emphasis is less on a two-person relationship with communicative potential than it is on a process whereby barriers to self-knowledge in one central character are removed. In these works, the pattern of the journey of the mythic hero – as explicated in Joseph Campbell's *The Hero with a Thousand Faces* – is somewhat apparent. A hero receives a 'call' to adventure, is tested, undergoes initiation, experiences apotheosis, and returns to the world. The pattern is one of disintegration, enlightenment and enhanced reintegration. The shorter plays *Reunion* and *The Shawl* comprise a special group of two plays in which just the last two stages of that pattern are shown, and more emphasis is placed on a burgeoning relationship that is its end possibility. In each case this relationship is not between two males, but between an older man and a younger woman. In *Reunion*, they are blood-related: a long-separated father and daughter. In all these plays, dialogue and structure deftly orchestrate the characters' hesitant approaches to each other.

Edmond and *The Verdict* were worked on at much the same time and have several similarities, including a focus, unusual for Mamet, on one character, rather than a pair. Each work takes the form of a journey through a blighted landscape and has strong allegorical overtones. The 'hero' casts aside a mask, sets out on a journey with a purpose, almost disintegrates with the pressures of the new 'zone' he has entered, achieves enlightenment, and returns to a state in which he can share his new insights. In their unenlightened states, the two protagonists have even worked for the same archetypal bourgeois firm, which Mamet calls 'Stearns and Harrington'.

Though *The Verdict* is an adaptation of a novel by Barry Reed, it is justifiable to deal with it at some length in a consideration of Mamet's work, because, unlike the earlier adaptation of *The Postman Always Rings Twice*, there are major differences from the source. Mamet alters the structure of events leading up to the climactic courtroom trial, and alters the import of the resolution. He adds three major characters, omits another, and alters the names and characteristics of another two. In Barry Reed's hands, *The Verdict* is a rousing story of an underdog lawyer winning out against a Bostonian professional aristocracy; in Mamet's and Sidney Lumet's hands it is a parable of a man's moral regeneration and renewal of faith.

At the outset Joe Galvin (Paul Newman) is an aging, booze-ridden 'ambulance-chaser' lawyer who shuttles between dingy bars and funeral parlours and his dilapidated office. Later we learn that he has evolved his present role of compromised survivor because of moral integrity too fine for his surroundings. When he protested at his law firm's strategy of bribing a juror in one of his cases, they had him jailed; when he withdrew the protest, he was released. But the firm sacked him; and his wife, daughter of the senior partner, divorced him. A mentor and ex-partner, Mick Morrissey, passes on to him a malpractice suit against a Roman Catholic hospital. Doctors gave the wrong anaesthetic to a pregnant woman; this brought on brain damage, and she is now a living vegetable. Morrissey gives Galvin the case as a financial favour, because it is likely to be settled out of court. But, after Galvin sees the client, he 'hears the call' and decides to bring the case to trial. Though Morrissey stands by him, he suffers a series of setbacks that test him to the uttermost. The plaintiff's working-class relatives are furious that he has rejected the proffered out-of-court settlement. His star witness, a colleague of the accused doctors, is bought off by the rival law firm. The presiding judge, in the pocket of powerful but unspecified downtown interests, refuses to give him more time to realign his strategy. Worst of all, Laura Fischer (Charlotte Rampling), a woman he has met at his favourite bar and become involved with, turns out to be a spy for the rival firm, planted to worm information out of him. All of this does not deflect him from his purpose; and he wins when he unearths a surprise witness who gives evidence that the doctors falsified crucial information on the patient's admission chart.

Galvin takes arms against the moral turpitude of a world of which, at the outset, he is a casualty – a world mildewed by 'business' corruption and venality. The chief identifiable villains in Mamet's eyes are the professional classes –

doctors and lawyers. Doneghy, one of the plaintiff's relatives, tells Galvin that he and his kind really do not care about their working-class clients:

> You guys, you guys, you're all the same. The Doctors at the *Hospital*, *you* . . . it's 'What I'm going to do for you'; but you screw up it's 'We did the best that we could. I'm dreadfully sorry . . .' And people like me live with your mistakes the rest of our lives.[1]

A tough older nurse tells Galvin later that doctors and lawyers have 'no *loyalty* . . . no nothing . . . you're a bunch of whores'. Mamet suggests as well that corruption goes beyond specific social sources, that it includes an almost metaphysical element. Morrissey tells Laura about the past incident of Galvin's jailing and that the doors opened 'as if by magic' when he told his firm that he would retract his protest. Morrissey refers to the ace rival lawyer, Concannon, as the 'Prince of Fuckin' *Darkness*' because of his legerdemain over juries, witnesses and resources. One critic even saw a connection between the red motif in the cinematography and Satanism, and noted that, when Laura first appears, she wears a red scarf.[2] Certainly, Andrej Bartkowiak's visual evocation of the Boston through which Galvin moves – dirty snow, greying buildings, subdued but threatening reds and browns – accentuates a sense of pervasive unease which is not attributable to social causes alone.

In his opening address at the trial, though 'performing' for a jury, Galvin is describing his own moral journey through trial towards redemption. The social conviction of Galvin's words are counterpointed by the low-key uncertainty with which they are delivered in the film:

You know, so much of the time we're lost. We say 'Please, God, tell us what is right. Tell us what's true. There is no justice. The rich win, the poor are powerless . . .' We become tired of hearing people lie. After a time we become dead. A little dead. We start thinking of ourselves as victims.

(*Pause.*)

And we *become* victims

(*Pause.*)

And we *become* weak . . . and *doubt* ourselves, and doubt our institutions . . .

He then reminds the jury that, on that day, they are the law – 'not some *book*, and not the *lawyers*', and, if 'we would have faith in *justice*, we must only believe in *ourselves*. (*Beat.*) And *act* with justice.' Galvin's lack of assurance in delivering these apparently assured words is an indication of uncertainty, of a lack of ease in his social role. Paul Newman underlined this in his performance through a kind of nervous hesitation, an overriding diffidence. This Galvin is verbally assured only when he is telling jokes to cronies in a bar or when manipulating clients who are clearly his social inferiors. Later, with Laura, he is flummoxed and inarticulate under the pressure of drink, intimacy and the shadow of almost certain failure. But Mamet suggests that Galvin ultimately succeeds because of, not in spite of, his vulnerability. Several times, at the end of his apparent resources, he asks people to help him. His ex-partner and the young ex-nurse who gives decisive courtroom testimony respond positively.

Any Campbell-like pattern of reintegration is qualified by moral ambivalence, so that the characteristic Mamet dialectic is in operation. This also saves the film from being a simple social parable on the lines of earlier films such as

those of Frank Capra. Ambivalence is apparent in the
verdict itself, which involves a financial award greater than
what was asked for, and makes Galvin and his cause look
greedy; and it is also apparent in the lack of resolution of
the relationship with Laura. As in *Edmond*, a major
subsidiary motif is sexual exploitation, here of the man by
the woman. But Laura is a much more complex character
than her counterpart in the novel, who is exposed as a spy
earlier in the game and whose affair with Galvin is less
significant. We learn that she has been married to a lawyer
and is qualified in law herself. Concannon, in trying to ease
her conscience, tells her that to make a professional
comeback and set up a practice to serve the needy she, like
they, will have to win the larger cases by fair means or foul –
for only by so doing can a firm afford *pro bono* work for the
poor. Laura, wracked by guilt, wants Galvin to win in spite
of her professional brief. She sets up a date in a restaurant
with Galvin in which she clearly intends to confess to him.
She also invites her own exposure by leaving her pay
cheque from Concannon in a half-open handbag.
Morrissey finds it, and tips Galvin off when he is on his way
to meet her. In one of the film's most powerful scenes, he
enters the posh restaurant and sees her sitting at a table; she
realises that he knows; then he goes to her and, wordlessly,
knocks her to the floor. At the end, possibilities for the
affair are still held out. She tries to phone Galvin, and he
refuses to answer it. But we sense that his resilience will
crumble, and that she will keep trying. The 'positive'
ending of *The Verdict* still leaves it a moot point how
generously Galvin will be able to act to those who have
betrayed him in the past – even with his newly-won
self-knowledge and confidence.

   Though *The Verdict* was very well received, some critics
disliked the fuzziness in Mamet's and Lumet's indictment

of specific causes of social corruption. A similar criticism was levelled at the darker-toned and more allegorical *Edmond*.

In *Edmond*, the hero leaves his wife to achieve liberation from the excessive routine, responsibility and constriction of his life. After being thwarted and defrauded in a whole series of deals for satisfying sex, he aggressively goes on the offensive, and kicks a black pimp unconscious or dead, beds a waitress in a one-night stand, kills her with a knife in a quarrel, goes to jail, and ends up in a homosexual bond with a black cell-mate.

Mamet insists that this fable encompasses the disintegration and reintegration of a personality who feels resentment against women, blacks and homosexuals and does not understand that letting out such hostilities in action is a 'false dawn' to a genuine liberation. 'Every fear hides a wish', says Edmond in his cell; he finds during his harrowing journey that he is attracted to some of the things that he most fears. At the end, in Mamet's view, Edmond's 'sexual identity, his social identity, his racial identity have been fractured and discarded. What he says is "I didn't need them anyhow. I'm so happy that none of these can be taken from me ever again." '[3] Later Mamet described the play as being

> about a man trying to come to grips with his life in a society which he cannot understand and cannot support. It's time to go back, examine his roots, to examine his actions in the past and try to begin to address, legitimately, things over which he has been confused or upset. Or repressed for a number of years.[4]

Mamet presents Edmond's journey as a fable-like allegory, but it is qualified by ironies. The allegorical pattern can be connected with German Expressionism and with Joseph Campbell. The characters have mostly generic names, except for Edmond Burke himself – a symbolic tie-in to the author of *The Vindication of Natural Society*! The titles of the brief scenes, and the necessarily minimalist staging used in Mosher's production, suggest 'stations' on a journey of the soul. These satirically correspond to the methods that a bar acquaintance suggests Edmond might use to free himself from social constriction: '*Pussy* . . . *Power* . . . *Money* . . . uh . . . *adventure* . . . uh, *self-destruction* . . . uh, *religion* . . . release, uh, ratification'. Then there is the affiliation with Campbell. No other Mamet play so clearly reveals the influence on him of *The Hero with a Thousand Faces*. Campbell explicates a mythic pattern in which the hero hears a call to adventure, heeds it after hesitation, crosses into a special zone, receives an initiation through a series of trials in which 'to hear and profit . . . one may have to submit somehow to purgation and surrender', and finally reaches an apotheosis in which 'we no longer desire and fear; we are what was desired and feared', at which point a return to enhanced reintegration can be made.[5]

Bigsby suggests that such affiliations are ironic, and that '*Edmond* is an ironic *Bildungsroman* in that its protagonist sets out on a quest for self-knowledge and experience which leaves him baffled and imprisoned'. Once dissatisfied as a bourgeois husband constrained by routine and responsibility, he has in the final scene 'been coerced into a relationship that makes him the "wife" of his fellow inmate. He has simply reversed the roles of the first part of the play and is now more absolutely trapped in a smaller room than the one he had once sought to escape.'[6] As we shall see, it is difficult to accept the validity of Bigsby's reading.

Another affiliation useful for pinpointing the play's structural peculiarities, suggested by Robert Brustein, is with Büchner's *Woyzeck*.[7] There is a coexistence both of 'fate' and human causality. Edmond decides to embark on his journey after a visit to a fortune-teller. She tells him in Scene 1 that he is special and not where he belongs. She announces, 'And you are unsure what your place is. To what extent you are cause and to what an effect . . . .' Initially, Edmond is a man who takes action to move beyond his constricting social role and experience something deeper in his nature, even at terrible personal cost. Later, as a result of that choice, he is sometimes the victim of forces over which he has no control. As in Büchner's play, some of the scenes in *Edmond* could take place in any order; others are presented as a cause-and-effect series, but the effects are sometimes frighteningly out of proportion to the causes, notably in the murder scene.

Campbell's allegorical pattern provides the most illuminating guide with which to examine Mamet's intentions in the play. Edmond's journey falls into three stages roughly consonant with the three 'phases' of the journey of Campbell's hero: departure, initiation and return. Edmond hears the 'call' through the fortune-teller. His 'departure' from the familiar first leads him through the one-upmanship of 'business', then into aggressive violence and sex, as he becomes the perpetrator and then the victim of one-sided sex scenarios; then he moves into contemplative territory where he can examine his past and understand what has driven him, so that in the end communion and a kind of reintegration are in sight.

At the beginning, Edmond is buttoned-down in a social role that gives him no satisfaction or even a voice that is his own. After he leaves his wife, the ensuing scenes show him in a series of 'business' transactions for sex which leave him hopelessly outmanoeuvred. They are initiated by a conversation with a man in a bar, who advises him to go and 'get laid'. This appears to be a 'personal' encounter, but in fact even it is a transaction. The man buys him a drink so he will '*remember* there was something who listened', even though the man has done most of the talking. Thereafter, Edmond becomes the 'mark' in encounters with a bar-girl, a peep-show girl, a brothel-manager, a whore, a card-sharper and a pawnbroker. His middle-class 'business' notions of being 'straight' have no relevance in this netherworld of predators; but the tone of the play is still mordant, and Edmond so far is seen as a comic victim.

The second stage of his journey, his arrival into a different territory of self-development, comes when he speaks to an unknown woman on a subway platform: 'My mother had a hat like that . . . She wore it for years. She had it when I was a child'. The remark is significant in two ways. It is not a counter in a duel for dominance, a come-on for sexual favours, or an opener in a 'business' transaction; as a reference to Edmond's own past it is the first sign that he is beginning to examine his roots. But the woman moves off coldly, and this unleashes his first outburst of furious anger, in which he abuses her. In the next scene, this anger gets an even fuller release as he bashes the black pimp who attempts to mug him. Then in the next scene, brimming over with a sense of release, he picks up the waitress Glenna in a coffee-house.

Structurally, the scene with Glenna after they have had sex forms the centrepiece of the play. Here, like Brecht's *Galy Gay*, Edmond finds another social mask to wear, swapping the one of bourgeois businessman for that of liberated fighter–stud. The mask will not fit, and must be discarded, with murderous consequences. The scene is possibly Mamet's most scabrous condemnation of the life-denying constrictions of the one-sided sex scenario, and this time (unlike in *The Verdict*) , it is the man and not the woman who is the sexual exploiter. After the sex, which apparently has left them unsatisfied, Edmond tries to give the encounter 'meaning' by casting Glenna into a prescribed image, which she resists. He wants her to be 'who she is', as he has lately tried to be who he is, so that together they can change their lives. His notion of her is the same as society's designation of her job role. 'Say it: I am a waitress', he bullies her, proving the extent to which he is still in thrall to such definitions. She, for her part, is what she wants to be: an actress. He rejects this because she has not yet appeared in New York in front of a paying audience. She then gets violently angry, and in rejecting Edmond in turn she perhaps falsely insists that all she saw in him to start with was a sex partner: 'WHAT DID I DO, PLEDGE MY LIFE TO YOU? I LET YOU FUCK ME. GO AWAY.' As she panics, he ironically equates madness with self-indulgence – and stabs her to death. Afterwards he blames her for this: '*now* look what you've done'. Then it is his turn to be cast into uncongenial roles in others' scenarios. Just as he is about to discharge his responsibility for murder onto born-again religion, he is spotted by the woman on the subway, who tells a policeman that 'He tried to rape me on the train', and he is arrested. Afterwards, when Edmond is in prison for the murder, his black cell-mate orders him, 'I think you should just get on my body', and he is forced to comply.

Until this scene, Mamet's use of language in *Edmond* is closely allied to the first two phases of Edmond's journey. His mask at the beginning constricts and distorts his talk, which comes out a constipated mixture of monosyllabic rejoinders and polysyllabic hand-me-downs from newsmagazines and business get-togethers. When he discusses sex, he whispers, uses euphemisms, or talks in clichés. 'You don't interest me spiritually or sexually', he tells his wife. 'My wife and I are incompatible', he tells the man in the bar. 'I'd like to have intercourse with you', he informs the whore. But, in his second phase, he finds a new voice with a vengeance. After the violence against the pimp, his words are freed, his sentences become staccato bursts of certitude, peppered with four-letter words. He thinks he now knows who he is, that his new mask is his 'real self' that has re-emerged after years of repression. Like Teach's, however, this stream of verbal dexterity actually justifies the amorality, violence and hatred that he thinks has liberated him. Glenna is overwhelmed and stifled by the verbal flood. Like Deb in *Sexual Perversity in Chicago*, she innately distrusts words and does not believe they mean what they say. 'What does it mean if I say something?' she protests when Edmond insists that she define herself as waitress. Edmond retains his new-found verbal fluency right up to the scenes in prison; although even before his sexual humiliation the words show signs of short-circuitry, flowing back on one another, ending in pauses, non-sequiturs and repetitions. In the scene with the Chaplain, Edmond's inarticulacy reaches its nadir, as he is asked why he killed Glenna and cannot complete his sentence:

> I . . . (*Pause.*) I . . . (*Pause.*) *I don't . . . I . . . I don't*
> . . . (*Pause.*) I . . . (*Pause.*) I don't . . . (*Pause.*) *I* don't
> . . . (*Pause.*) I don't think . . . (*Pause.*) I . . . (*Pause.*)
> (*The* CHAPLAIN *helps* EDMOND *up and leads him to the door.*)

Now the final phase of Edmond's journey is manifested

in closely linked action and dialogue. In the penultimate scene, he is shown writing a letter to the mother of a girl he took to the formal high school graduation dance. Remembering the past, he confesses that it was perhaps necessary for him to think that the girl went unwillingly with him – and then he realises that he does not really believe this. In this scene, he deeply examines his past experience, so much so that he feigns illness to get rid of a visitor. In Mosher's production, Colin Stinton projected a vulnerability that he had not shown anywhere else in the play.

While some critics found the final scene difficult to accept in the way Mamet had intended, it reinforces Edmond's new-found vulnerability and indicates further growth in him. Though the relationship with the cell-mate was initiated by threat, it is now clearly an authentic one marked by genuine rapport – and this latter condition is clearly indicated in the language. It overlaps but moves in consonant rhythms. It is not an instance of a parallel monologue. The men anticipate each other's thoughts, so that in spite of their differences they are in tune with each other. This is indicated in the dots before some of the lines, which here indicates an easy flow between the speakers. The men talk about special knowledge, special insights about human life and its secret causes that might be known to hermits, shamans, men who like them live isolated from society and hence are prone to introspection and wonder, no matter how ironically bestowed. Animals too have this knowledge:

PRISONER.　. . . Maybe they're *animals* . . .
EDMOND. Yes.
PRISONER. That were *left* here . . .
EDMOND. *Aeons* ago.

PRISONER. *Long* ago . . .

EDMOND. . . . and have *bred* here . . .

PRISONER. Or maybe *we're* the animals . . .

EDMOND. . . . Maybe we are . . .

PRISONER. *You* know, how they, *they* are supreme on their . . .

EDMOND. . . . Yes.

PRISONER. On their *native* world . . .

EDMOND. But when you put them here.

PRISONER. *We* say they're only *dogs*, or *animals*, and *scorn* them . . .

EDMOND. . . . Yes.

PRISONER. We scorn them in our fear. But . . . don't you think? . . .

EDMOND. . . . It very well could be . . .

PRISONER. But on their native *world* . . .

EDMOND. . . . Uh-huh . . .

PRISONER. . . . they are *supreme* . . .

EDMOND. I think that's very . . .

PRISONER. And what *we* have done is to disgrace ourselves.

EDMOND. We have.

PRISONER. Because we did not treat them with respect.

In the script, the description of the kiss that ends the scene is characteristically terse: 'EDMOND *gets up, goes over and exchanges a goodnight kiss with the* PRISONER. *He then returns to his bed and lies down.*' In Mosher's production, the kiss was intense, with a searching look indicative of deep love and affection; but the final image was of Edmond alone, sitting on the edge of the double-decker bunk, with the partner sleeping above. This peaceful image suggested the contemplation of a void, the 'ultimate boon' for him who can know himself by managing to 'tear the coverings away'.[8] From the evidence of Mosher's production, the relationship between Edmond and his cell-mate has more value than that with the wife, with its robotinised hostility. In Scene 2 with her, though free to go, Edmond was hopelessly constricted in his social role and his three-piece suit. Now, simply clad in loose-fitting whites, he is imprisoned – but at peace, learning about himself, and involved in a communing relationship with another human being – and this outweighs all the qualifying ironies.

The chief of these, of course, is that Edmond can only achieve the 'introspection and wonder' needed for genuine self-discovery in prison – after his path through society's stations of purgatory. Even more intensely than Galvin in *The Verdict*, Edmond moves alone through a bare, vitiated world of which he was part; unlike the world of *The Verdict*, it is one in which corruption and death of the spirit is too pervasive at every level – personal, institutional, sociological – for any causes to be clearly identified.

In *Lone Canoe, or, The Explorer*, Mamet likewise deals with a 'hero' who undergoes a testing journey and arrives at a deeper self-understanding. The explorer Fairfax, lost in the frozen north, lives with the Indian tribe which nurtured him back to health, and takes a wife. Found by his friend VanBrandt, who has led several earlier search expeditions for him in vain, Fairfax is only persuaded to return to London with VanBrandt when told that he is in disgrace because of a diary which has implicated him in the death of some of his men. As he is leaving, he fires at the shaman to protect VanBrandt, who is wounded. On the voyage south, he finds evidence in a journal that he has been tricked – that it is in fact VanBrandt who is in disgrace, for the incompetent failure of the rescue expeditions. Fairfax thinks he has killed the shaman, but nevertheless returns to the tribe to face the penalty of death by torture. The shaman has not died, and Fairfax is reunited with the tribe and its hard life.

While the play follows the pattern of departure, initiation and return, the significance of all Fairfax's choices are undercut by the circumstances. The first – to desert his late home and return to London – is made because of false evidence. The second – to return to the tribe – is neutralised by his losing the way south, VanBrandt dying of wounds, and the shaman not dying. The whole 'journey of the hero' is mostly activated by the melodramatic machinations of VanBrandt. *Lone Canoe* is lacking in the paradoxes and dialectical ironies which give distinctiveness to much of Mamet's other work – including plays like *Edmond* which depend heavily on 'fable' models. The play is beset with a kind of banality which may be the result of a too-literal application of Bettelheim and Campbell. The dialogue has something of the portentousness, but little of the lyricism, that marks the prose style of Campbell. Following its disastrous Goodman premiere, Mamet did not publish *Lone Canoe*; he has said that he intends to work on it further.

In *Reunion* and *The Shawl*, both short plays but among Mamet's most individual works, closeness develops between an older man and a younger woman. It cannot take hold, however, until the man receives an insight or makes a decision which allows him to consolidate an earlier process of self-growth – a process which roughly parallels the 'journeys' of the protagonists of *The Verdict* and *Edmond*. In *Reunion*, the two are actually a long-separated father and daughter. In *The Shawl* the relationship is more elusive but builds between a 'professional' and his client.

For the 1977 and 1979 productions, *Reunion* was preceded by a ten-minute curtain-raiser, *Dark Pony*, which is thematically related to the longer play and provides a comparison with it. In a car on a homeward journey, a father tells his five-year-old daughter the story of the Indian brave Rain Boy and his Dark Pony. One night in winter, Rain Boy is set upon by a pack of wolves; in the nick of time, Dark Pony arrives, saves him, and brings him back to life. Telling this reassuring fable does not quite promote the contact it promises. The encounter should cement the bond between father and daughter, and the father's position as provider of protection and banisher of fears; but Mamet's production, and close examination of the text, suggest that the story has only imperfect efficacy. True, the child moves from fear and tiredness to comfort, and a greater awareness of the world outside the car; the sound of the road tells her that they are almost home. But the father becomes increasingly self-absorbed and isolated; he seems to identify with, and magnify, certain details in the story at the expense of the whole. His last line repeats the cry of the brave at the time of his greatest danger and distress: '(*to self*) Dark Pony, / Rain Boy calls to you'; and earlier he has intoned Rain Boy's desperate accusation, 'You have forgotten me', as if relating the brave's dilemma to some unspoken one of his own. What is implied is that, in spite of the intimacy of the protected environment, the father and little daughter have essentially missed contact. They have crossed past each other in contrary directions to become isolated once again.

In *Reunion*, the difficulties of the relationship between an older father and daughter are immensely more complex, but the need of the characters for contact is greater, as they have been separated for twenty years. Bernie left home in the early 1950s and has not seen his daughter since; Carol, now twenty-four, married to a much older man, suddenly felt the need to know her father and initiated the meeting through her husband. It takes place in Bernie's modest apartment and, after the embarrassed accord of its first moments, opens up many differences. Bernie and Carol are now members of different classes, with different temperaments, ambitions and philosophies.

Bernie has reached hard-won tranquillity by undergoing his own 'journey', involving disintegration of an old self and reintegration of a new one. He has walked out of a marriage; for no definite purpose, and for no apparent reason other than that his life was getting into deeper disarray through drinking. His own 'trials' have come in the failure of a second marriage, further descent into alcoholism, being fired from a job he was proud of, and estrangement from most of his relatives. This odyssey has, however, brought about only a limited enlightenment. He has stabilised his life, found a restaurant job he likes, and is contemplating marriage once again; but this does not really constitute an enhanced reintegration. He does see that his previous vagaries have been 'looking for a way around', and so knows that lack of willingness to take responsibility has been behind much of his earlier past; he has developed a strange philosophy in which one has to 'Take a chance', and 'grab' one's chance for happiness, but at the same time one always has to 'Pay the price./Always the price. Whatever it is./And you gotta know it and be prepared to pay it if you don't want it to pass you by.' Out of this emerges little more than the old saw 'Don't bite off more than you can chew', and this explains his sense of the diminution of the possibilities open to him. Even in looking back on the past and trying to justify leaving two separate families, he falls back on the excuse 'These things happen'; and this is not far from the old saw 'Life goes on', which, just before the climax of the play, Carol angrily challenges. But all this gives Bernie some sort of grounding. It fits his view of himself as a working man, 'Ex-this./Ex-that', who is proud of his Second World War record as a tail gunner and his job as a skilled line-repair man. He has no further prospect for upward mobility, and he does not desire it.

Carol, however, is educated into middle-class values and is upwardly mobile. When Bernie remarks that she takes good care of herself, she tersely replies, 'Got to.' She took the initiative in finding Bernie, and is actively involved in changing her life and in realising her possibilities. During the encounter, we learn how deep her dissatisfaction is with her life; though materially quite well-off, she is cramped spiritually and physically. She reveals to Bernie that her husband makes use of her in an office job she dislikes, her stepsons barely tolerate her, and her marital sex life has petered out. While Mamet implies that she has married a man nearly twice her age as a father-substitute, she blames Bernie for her present condition: 'It's got to have affected my marriage . . . / I come from a Broken Home. / The most important institution in America.' Even though she blames Bernie, she is desperately hoping for a connection with him that will replenish her.

The dialogue is a barometer of whether the characters are hiding behind social roles or lowering them. There are bursts of confident fluency in between stretches of halting rhythmic uncertainty. Although Bernie has most of the lines in the play and Carol is comparatively silent, her non-verbal responses to Bernie's words, sparsely indicated in the printed text, are crucial. As in some other Mamet plays where the dialogue is unevenly divided, especially Scene 1 of *The Woods*, the reticent character is testing the more voluble one – and the voluble one knows it. Carol's silences are expectant, even demanding; she hangs on Bernie's words, and he reacts by talking at times out of nervous panic. He slips into banalities, repetitions, and only seems to find relief in some stories he tells about his past. Here he can find coherence and a comparative sense of security. While the two major stories he tells about his past make him appear vulnerable and pathetic, they do fulfil what Carol expects about their relationship, for she tells him at the climax that she wants to hear his 'goddamn war stories and the whole thing'. As far as Bernie is concerned, his words cover a fear that he cannot give her what she wants, and the telling of the stories convinces him that the answers to the problems of their relationship lie not in the past, but in the present.

The structure of the play consists of a series of halting moves towards greater communion. Some comically backfire. Bernie talks of her baby pictures, says that he looks at them 'constantly', and then cannot find them. He offers her coffee, she says she would prefer tea; and then, in a bit of business included in Mamet's production but not printed in the text, he absent-mindedly gives her coffee anyway. The greatest barrier to more genuine intimacy is broken when they have an argument. He objects to her notion that he is 'wasted' in his restaurant job, an opinion she bases on her childhood idealisation of him as an Indian brave. He takes it as mere middle-class snobbery, and says that the way she has been brought up, 'though all very well and good . . . is not basically my life . . . / I mean, you haven't even *been* to the restaurant, for chrissakes . . .'. This unleashes a defensive, angry outburst from her – and, in Lamont Johnson's TV cable presentation of Mamet's production, Carol crossed to the window and let fresh air into the room at that point.[9]

Now comes a major attack by Carol on Bernie's 'Life goes on' philosophy, which she equates with her husband's. It apparently gives Bernie new insight, a new determination to change. In theory, he knows already that living in the present is more important than living in the past: 'The actions are important. / The present is important . . . / . . . you've gotta be where you are. / . . . While you're there. / Or you're nowhere.' But one can live actively or passively in the present; one can sit back and say, 'Life goes on', or one can take action now effectively to change things. Bernie now determines to do the latter:

> BERNIE. . . . let's get up, go out, do this, go look at the locomotive if they've still got it there, something . . . you know?
>
> Because, all kidding aside, what's between us isn't going nowhere, and the rest of it doesn't exist.

It is of small moment that this doctrine of present action is ironically exemplified by a trip down memory lane to look at a locomotive – for Bernie's newly-expressed resolve to do something cues Carol to come right out with her expectations. This forms the climax of the play. She confesses that she has always felt cheated never having a father, and that she does not want to be just 'pals and buddies', but wants him to be her father. 'I'm entitled to it', he says. 'Am I? / Am I?', and he replies, 'Yes.'

In spite of this new resolution, Bernie backslides, perhaps scared by the very vehemence of her demands. He instinctively shies away from a dinner alone with Carol; she has to insist on their going alone, without her husband in tow. There is a final *faux pas* similar to the incidents with the photos and coffee. Bernie gives her a gift of a gold bracelet. It was meant to be inscribed with her birthdate, but the inscription is incorrect, because, according to Bernie, 'my threes look like eights'. But, unlike Nick in *The Woods*, Carol accepts the gift.

The meeting with Carol apparently completes a process of reintegration in Bernie; after his departure from home, his severing himself from Carol and her mother, his long odyssey of 'trial' with alcoholism and failure is finally given a chance for a rounded close.

The Shawl is a small but rich work which plays for about an hour. It combines the protégé–mentor motif with that of the bond between an older man and a younger woman. The play is set in the 'office' of John, a genteel but impoverished 'mystic'. A woman in her late thirties, Miss A, is visiting him. She wants to contact her dead mother, to decide whether to contest her will, and to find out why her mother left her nothing. In the next scene, John's 'professional' integrity and loyalty to his client is challenged by his new assistant and lover Charles, who wants him to persuade Miss A to contest the will and give them the fortune. John ultimately refuses and at the end of the play sits with Miss A and draws her deeper into confidence in his powers, which seem, in a surprise ending, to be marked by genuine prescience.

The play is structurally 'well made', and there are three effective reversals – but once again there is a significant alternative structure that has thematic weight. There are five scenes which contrast the quality of two differing relationships; and the central scene, a seance, is like the apex of a pyramid in which the three characters are onstage together for the only time, and in which the relationships intersect. John is here faced with people antagonistic to one another – rivals for his allegiance.

The bond between John and Charles is one of the mentor–protégé, but it is also overtly homosexual. As in the plays dealing with heterosexual relationships, the lovers' relations are twisted by power-plays and one-sided fantasy scenarios. Charles seems to have a hustler's obsession with himself as a commodity; but he is also fascinated by John's 'profession', especially since it seems to touch on privileged knowledge. In the second scene, John explains to Charles that his skills are actually based on scientific observation and inference: throwing out cues, gauging micro-responses in the eyes and body, thus gaining clients' trust and 'suggesting' more information out of them. John stresses that research is necessary between sessions, that known facts have to be capitalised on. He also stresses that there is an elusive, intuitive skill involved, and that at times he has to make a leap in the dark. John gives Charles a demonstration of his skill relating to facts about Charles's past that he could not have known – he reveals that he inadvertently came by them in going through Charles's wallet for a tip. Charles is offended, and doubts the legitimacy of John's 'profession' when he is shown the trick 'from the back'. So he impatiently gives John an ultimatum: to bilk Miss A of her inheritance – or lose him.

The bond that develops between Miss A and John, on the other hand, is enriched by ever-increasing trust, and by mutual respect for the primacy of the intuitive and the mysterious. Their rapport recalls that of Edmond and the black cell-mate, and the final conversation in that play about the privileged knowledge that certain people can develop in isolation from society. In the first scene, John insists to Miss A that certain 'powers' exist, and that she knows they can be known. She, like him, has 'psychic' ability. Though this moment is qualified in the next scene, when John tells Charles that such remarks are mere strategy, the rhythms suggest an authenticity which goes beyond strategy with this particular client. In an echo of *Edmond*, Mamet has John say,

> For we say 'knowledge,' what is it? It is our attempt to be part of something which continues. Which we *are*

part of. And *fear* – what is it? We fear that thing that
we wish does not exist. But we know it exists. Don't
we? (*Pause*.)

MISS A. I don't know.

JOHN. Yes, you *do*. For what has brought you here? That
knowledge. That there is a hidden order in the world.

Miss A, for her part, wants to know what went wrong in her
closeness with her dead mother. As John later tells
Charles, she wants to know, first, whether she should
contest the will; why the will did not include her; and, most
important, why her mother did not have unalloyed love for
her. Events soon prove that even these questions are only
the tip of the iceberg – for John senses that she is troubled
and 'deeply repressed'. He begins to win her trust – and this
is partly because his profession is no 'business' to him. He
refuses Charles's demand that he use the $50 bill left at the
first meeting, signed 'in confidence'. He has faith that he
will be paid, and well; but only because Miss A will believe
that his services are worth it. In the final scene, he says to
her what he told Charles he would say: 'some, as they can
afford it, as they wished, might pay up to a thousand
dollars. To help us with our work. Some would leave fifty.
Some would leave nothing. It's completely up to you.' The
place of 'commodity exchange' in the relationship is
completely different from its place in the relationship
between John and Charles.

The quality of the encounters between John and Miss A
is indicated in the overlapping consonances of thought, the
anticipation of each other's wavelengths, the cues which
John skilfully throws to Miss A and which she seizes on.
Both have something to give to each other, and this is
reflected in the dialogue. By contrast, the encounters
between John and Charles are fraught with dissonance –

the overlapping and simultaneity are marked by challenging equivocation or impatience. Mamet, in this sparest of plays, is scrupulously careful about the rhythmic effects of overlapping speech; but, with each pair of characters, the overlapping has different consequences. With the men, it is guardedness or disruptive alienation; with John and Miss A, accord.

The seance scene intensifies John's involvement with Miss A, but, more importantly, Mamet here creates a rich evocation of the lyricism and mystery of the unknown which the play celebrates. Again, a dialectic operates – we know that what John does is partly based on a performance. John 'becomes' a medium, an 1840 Boston woman whose tale of passion and murder emerges like a weirdly surreal replay of some Hawthorne novella. Mamet once again displays his fascination for inserted 'story', and his brilliance in creating mesmerising rhythms and images for such set pieces. The climax of the scene reveals that John is indeed trying to fulfil Charles's demands. Miss A unexpectedly makes the greatest test of his powers by 'catching him out' over her 'photograph' of her mother on the table. He identifies it as a likeness of the woman he saw in his 'trance' – but it is fake. As she starts to heap him with scorn, he reinstates her trust in him by announcing, at the very end of the scene, a truth she recognises. He 'saw' the mother by Miss A's childhood bedside wearing a red shawl.

In the next scene with Charles, John makes a major choice. He demystifies the knowledge of the shawl itself – the source was an old photograph. But Charles also wants to know how John came by an additional detail given Miss A – that she lost it five years ago. John merely asserts that this was also a trick, without explaining it, and denies the prescience that Charles senses and that will be fully unveiled in the final scene: 'I TOLD YOU. IT WAS A

TRICK. IT WAS A *TRICK*. ARE YOU DEAF?' This assertion has an intensity that protests too much. It is an indication both that John's knowledge that the shawl was lost is not just a 'trick', and that to tell Charles that it is may be costing John more than he can bear. For this assertion, of course, is also Charles's dismissal. John has found the strength not to betray Miss A to keep Charles. The choice signals a change in John, a lowering of the mask, a journey into unknown personal territory for him which harbours the possibility of a major personal reconstitution.

In the final scene the closeness between 'mystic' and client is solidified. She begins to need him as a genuine 'psychic', but, more, as a psychologist and surrogate father; the situation is not so very far from that of *Reunion*. She arrives for the meeting early, and notices that John is distressed, but not why. She then announces that she has decided to contest the will, and asks how she might pay John – apparently a termination of their dealings with each other. But then she stays, because she needs him: 'You *contacted* her.'

Though it is still possible that Miss A's money is a magnet, Mamet hints that John needs Miss A as much as she needs him. At the very least, he needs her as proof of his professional skill and as a vehicle for the powers of intuition that he has kept from Charles. At the final curtain, these powers are again evidenced by his revelation that he knows Miss A burnt the shawl, in rage, by the water five years before. Mamet has called *The Shawl* 'my Twilight Zone episode',[10] and the ending does unveil the 'hidden order of the world'. More significantly, the 'hidden order' of Miss A's world is uncovered. John's revelation shows his profound intuition about Miss A, and the information opens up vistas on Miss A's past, of ambivalent hatred and jealousy of her mother, and of overdependence on her.

The power of John's prescience here can only be effected through a development of trust between him and his client; therefore it is not a 'trick' *dénouement*. It finally breaks through the last vestiges of Miss A's crisp social role and erases the final major barrier to communion between two people. This communion epitomises 'the substance of things hoped for, the evidence of things not seen'.

7
The Plays in
the Theatre

John Lee Beatty, who has frequently worked with Mamet, said in 1979, 'I love designing David's plays. His work comes alive only when it's on the stage. There's a dimension that doesn't come through when you're just reading it.'[1]

This dimension is elusive – the printed text of a Mamet play at first seems skeletal, even skimpy, for the playwright gives virtually nothing but a bald description of the place where the action is set and the words that the characters speak. This is in line with much modern practice in the printing of plays, but Mamet is as spare as Beckett or Pinter. He defends his minimalism on the grounds that, through what his characters say, his intentions as a playwright are sufficiently clear, and that any remaining ambiguities are intentional.[2] This chapter will concentrate on the theatrical challenges of staging Mamet. Steven Schachter's 1978 New York production of a play not so far dealt with, the fascinating 'American fable' *The Water Engine*, affords an example of the way one director successfully met these challenges.

Initially it appears that Mamet's minimalism opens up exciting creative initiative for directors, designers and actors. In the early plays, Mamet sometimes stressed the initiatives possible. For example, at the beginning of *The Duck Variations*, he states that '*Any blocking or business is at the discretion of individual actors and directors.*' Similarly in *Squirrels*: '*The characters should each be dressed as befits their station in life and occupation*', and '*specifics should be dictated further by the humor of the designer, director and actors*'. He gives the basic requirements of the setting, then adds, '*further elaboration here, too, is discretionary*'.

Close study of Mamet's minimalist aesthetic – as well as the texts themselves – reveals the proper discretionary limits of directorial choice. Mamet is especially critical of unnecessary decoration, given his attachment to the power of fable narrative. Particularly undesirable is the 'characterising' business of actors, epitomised in the 'way that a British actor can use a handkerchief fifty ways to illustrate things about the character'.[3] Worst of all are 'production values'. Mamet stresses that 'the *best* production is the *least* production. The best production takes place in the mind of the beholder. . . . "Production", or "Production values" is code for *forsaking the story*.'[4] The phrase clearly encompasses not only the kind of elaborate *mise en scène* which Grotowski defined as 'rich theatre', but also the proliferation of naturalistic detail. Mamet dislikes anything in production which smacks of 'aesthetic politics' – that is, stylistic experimentation with no genuine creative intent and nothing to say. This includes work which seems to celebrate emotion for emotion's sake, or work which in his opinion is unduly arcane, like the so-called performance-art movement of the early 1980s. Direct presentationalism – addresses to the audience, acknowledgement of its presence in the theatre, abrogation of the fourth wall – is rare in his plays. In short, 'The acting, the design, the direction should all consist only of that bare minimum necessary to put forward the action. Anything else is embellishment, and weakens the play.'[5]

Consideration of some scenic details from Mamet and Mosher productions reveals difficulties with this minimalism in practice – especially of drawing the line between necessity and embellishment. 'Necessity' at its extreme is illustrated by Beatty's set for *Reunion* in New York, which consisted only of a table and two chairs; or Mamet's staging of *The Woods* in Chicago, which eschewed all naturalistic and atmospheric lighting-effects. On the other hand, Michael Merritt's set for *The Shawl*, while evocatively spare, was a little more detailed. The 'office' of the text became an elegant converted living-room with three symmetrical apertures at the back curtained in blue, an octagonal table and two chairs centre, and a sideboard to stage right. There was a Turkish rug on the floor. Necessity or embellishment?

The same questions arise in a consideration of the acting. Concentrating on 'necessity' can sometimes result in a semaphoring of the obvious. Acting in a Mosher or Mamet production tends to be clean and direct, but at times in Mosher's work the concentration on a major point of emphasis in a beat, the refusal to indulge in 'busy' blocking or business, can seem a little bloodless. In delivery, both directors are careful to have the actors bring out the inherent rhythms in the lines, but Mosher has been criticised for an 'italicisation' of dialogue, which sometimes precludes spontaneity.[6] Needless to say, this is appropriate in plays where the characters have an imposed social mask, or are being guarded. There is a reliance on static visual tableaux, largely the result of paring down movement and business, in which the clarity of the characters' intent can project clearly, and in which the ironies of the characters' relationships can register with a minimum of naturalistic distraction. At the same time, both directors have devised carefully selected pieces of business which are not specified in the text and which might be considered as falling into the realm of 'characterising' embellishment. Mention has been made of Bernie's offering Carol coffee after she says she would prefer tea, in Mamet's production of *Reunion*. Another example is furnished by Mosher's production of *The Shawl*. During the final encounter between John and Charles, John attempts to keep control of his feelings by peeling and dividing an orange on a plate and eating it with meticulous scrupulousness; after Charles walks out, he goes to a decanter on the sideboard, pours a single slug into a shot-glass, and downs it.

There are two special problems in staging Mamet. The first relates to the scenic choices made. The stage setting will influence whether a play is interpreted by audiences and critics in terms more of realism or of allegory. And the setting will in turn affect whether or not the play seems 'episodic' in the theatre. Most important of all, there is the question of how director and actors choose to interpret and bring out the subtext, particularly as it relates to the reacting or reticent character. This last problem is crucial; any Mamet critic has to consider it carefully, and some critical interpretations of plays may well depend on the initiative of a given director in a given production.

The stage design has a very important bearing on the perceived 'realism' of Mamet's plays. Several critics have pointed to Mamet's plays as metaphors for the American condition rather than a literal interpretation of facets of urban American life. The stage design may be crucial in pointing to one interpretation or the other. For example, if the junkshop of *American Buffalo* is filled with the kind of objects that make it look like 'home' for the characters, the play may seem part of mainline American realism. Conversely, if the lighting is cold and the objects are placed and chosen to suggest ugly obsolescence, the play will appear a metaphorical critique of capitalism. As we have seen, the text of *The Duck Variations* delineates strongly contrasted temperaments and philosophies in the play's two old men. Gerald Gutierrez, in his production for the Acting Company in Saratoga, New York, pushed this further by using three-quarter masks, with the mouths of the actors exposed. So, while there was precise realism in the accents and intonations of the two men, the allegorical implications of the play and its formal basis of inspiration were stressed scenically. In *Edmond*, while the printed text indicates spare locations, Mosher's staging stressed the allegorical and expressionist rather than the realistic aspects of the play. Actors moved around basic furniture pieces to different areas of the stage for the different locations. There were two solid doors in the back walls of the set, and the walls formed three sides of a black, menacing square. The doors, which were of brown wood, could be banged open and closed to suggest the abruptness of the emphatic entrance and exit, the jagged quality of threat so important in the play. These doors were also adapted to form some items which appear to present difficult staging-problems, such as a plexiglass panel in a booth, which proves a major point of contention between Edmond and a peep-show girl.[7]

Differently realised settings for the same play also give an interesting insight into the play's interpretation at different times and in different places. For instance, one might expect that in England the metaphorical significance of Mamet's plays would have more impact than the realistic, if only because the local allusions would not be directly apparent to English audiences, and English actors, no matter how skilful, would not be able to render Mamet's dialogue with the same ease as Americans. But, certainly in the case of *Glengarry Glen Ross*, settings have played an important part in the differences of interpretation. Michael Merritt's set for Mosher's production stressed selective realism in both acts. In the Chinese restaurant, orientalism was emphasised a little, so that the set had a bizarrely grotesque quality. The second act was more literal. Hayden Griffin's set for Bryden worked somewhat differently. In Act I, the restaurant was slightly more run-of-the-mill; it suggested borrowed comfort, home away from home. But his Act II was almost expressionist in impact. The office looked out onto a plain white-brick surface. Light glared through slats in the boarded-up window and walls of the ransacked office, the whole suggesting bars in the cage which imprisoned the characters. Of the two designs, it was Griffin's which most strongly stressed the play's metaphorical implications.

A stage setting can also sometimes release theatrical potential not apparent in a text, or can counterpoise textual problems – though Mamet's plays rarely need this kind of help. *Squirrels* does need it – and received it in its Chicago production. John Paoletti and Mary Griswold provided a set which playfully emphasised some of the play's metaphors to allow for a more free-wheeling physical comedy than the text suggests by itself. The design incorporated elements of realism, with a set suggesting a cluttered office and including, for example, a real radiator, but centred on an image of a squirrel running rampant in an hour-glass, and costumes and make-up that were strongly stylised. Music by Alaric Jans provided underpinning for picturisation and business within this space.[8] Similarly, the ingenious handling of the onstage and backstage scenes in *A Life in the Theatre*, with the reversed image of the theatre auditorium seen on the cyclorama, gave not only formal cohesion but poetry to a play which, if cursorily read, gives the impression of a series of insubstantial and episodic skits. This kind of setting was devised by Michael Merritt for Mosher's first production.

Of course, the kind of stage setting used determines the fluidity in staging of any multi-scene play. In most productions of Mamet's plays, the strategy has been to minimise gaps between scenes, and frequently this has tended to contradict the 'episodic' impression conveyed by the printed page. In Albert Takazauckas' New York production of *Sexual Perversity in Chicago*, for instance, scene followed scene almost without a break – but a feeling of dislocation was none the less created because the settings for each location were minimal. *A Life in the Theatre*, *Lakeboat*, *The Water Engine* and *Edmond* all had important initial productions on unit sets which reduced the impression of the 'episodic' without betraying the incongruity of juxtaposition of some of the most important scenes. Frequently, area-lighting increased the fluidity of this kind of presentation. Indeed, it was sometimes used so that individual scenes overlapped. In *Edmond*, for instance, lighting was used both to create a feeling of vertigo and to establish a sense of sinister fatality which operated above the realm of human causality. It emphasised a pattern of circularity in Mosher's area-staging about the imprisoning space. Kevin Rigdon's high spotlights produced a cold, alienating chiaroscuro which lagged slightly behind the action: a scene would begin in darkness; only then would a light give what reassurance of definition it could. This is a stage equivalent of a cinematic device in which the sound of a new scene is heard asynchronously during blackness, or sometimes even before the final image of the previous scene has faded. The cinematic quality of action implied here also operates within Mamet plays in which he lets two strands of action, or more, operate simultaneously. In the short *Shoeshine*, for example, he virtually cross-cuts between two equally important action-strands; in *Glengarry Glen Ross*, he creates a feeling of near-chaos at one point in Act II where four actions (in the sense of playing out intentions) are operating at once; and in *The Water Engine* several action frames operate at once. These strategies become noticeable chiefly in performance. They ensure that identification with certain characters and moral dismay at their conduct – empathy and Brechtian alienation – operate together in the theatre in a complex and cumulative way. The audience has no time to interpose its judgement in time gaps between scenes in the manner of Brechtian theatre, as is sometimes implied in the plays' printed format.

But by far the most important area of directorial initiative in realising Mamet's scripts has to do with filling out, and pointing, the subtext. At one level, this involves just the legitimate fleshing-out of what sometimes seems a skimpy and unpromising skeleton. This applies more to some plays than others. On paper, *The Water Engine*, for example, appears underdeveloped. This impression proves false; the context behind the spare lines is such that the play opens out most suggestively in the theatre. Much of *A Life in the Theatre* looks humdrum on the page; the theatrical parody scenes, where Robert and John perform their repertory roles to unseen audiences, sometimes seem niggardly, strained and unfunny. In fact, they give directors a wonderful chance to parody not only old-fashioned dramaturgy and 'classic' plays, but also styles of acting and staging. The Chekhov take-off scene (Scene 11) in the hands of Gutierrez, for example, became a scene in which long, unmotivated pauses separated painfully trivial dilemmas over whether to open or close windows. The scene was made even more inconsequential and amusingly slow in pace by droning balalaika music and the proverbial cricket and night sounds which Chekhov so detested in Stanislavsky's productions of his plays. Gutierrez also put in an episode in which John spasmodically tore up a manuscript, in a parody of Treplev's suicide in *The Seagull*. Humour for educated theatre buffs, perhaps; but each of the other 'onstage' scenes, taking off Noel Coward's *What Price Glory?*, O'Neill's sea plays, *Danton's Death* and *Men in White*, offers opportunities for theatrical parody more comprehensive and hilarious than is apparent from the printed page. Thus Mamet's minimalism does incorporate – as any first-rate playwright's – the kinds of situations in which, though the text looks sparse, the staging will bloom.

Often in Mamet, the pointing of the subtext determines how an important scene will be interpreted by an audience. In these cases the director has to be concerned with the intention of a speaking character, the subtext of his words and their rhythm; and, even more problematic, the intent and feelings of the listening or reticent character.

Mamet has jocularly spoken of his attempts to evolve a 'Unified Field Theory' of theatre. The challenge to an audience to catch a speaker's intent depends heavily on achieving the correct speech rhythm in production. Mamet claims,

> As a playwright . . . what one sees as a member of the audience is the intention of the actor . . . Even more

than one hears the words, what one sees is the intention of the actor as a human being; what we see in any human being is the real intention, not their overlay and what they would try and have us believe, not their attempts to manipulate us, but their real intention, and that the real intention of a person is always expressed in the rhythm of their speech. So . . . you . . . can delineate the intention by correctly delincating the rhythm of the speech.[9]

This theory partly explains his scrupulous attention to the rhythmic structure of the dialogue, repetitions, simultaneous delivery, overlapping, cut-ins, incomplete sentences, pronunciation oddities, and the presence in the middle of sentences of non-verbal exclamatory sounds. The theory also implies that the rhythm of sentences might uncover intentions which counterpoint the overt meaning of the words. For sound and rhythm to uncover any given character's intent, the rhythms must be scrupulously rendered in performance, which means an attention to dynamic markings by directors and actors analogous to those needed by musicians in scores by Schoenberg or Elliott Carter. Mamet is wryly aware that this can never be guaranteed. Even an attentive reader is apt to miss the implied rhythms of printed words and sentences. According to Meisner and Mamet's principles of acting, a performer plays 'the moment', and his rhythms are affected by how his partners in the scene react. It is sometimes very difficult in a Mamet script to work out how a given character may be reacting to a more dominant or talkative one – or how this may feed back to the speaker and thus affect his rhythms in turn. In a group of characters, it may not be certain who is listening and who is not, or whether the speaker is aware of such reactions. These ambiguities can remain unresolved in a reading of the play or in a radio

performance; they *must* be resolved one way or another
when the play is staged, by the very nature of theatrical
performance.

The problem can be broadly illustrated by the short play
Prairie du Chien (1979). Here a major motif, and a major
determinant in the play's impact and meaning, is a story
told and heard (or not heard) by other characters present in
the space. There are two strands of action occurring
simultaneously in the box car of a train speeding through
the Wisconsin night. In one, a storyteller spins a tale of
sexual jealousy, murder and the supernatural to a young
father with a sleeping child. In the other, two men play
cards, one finally accuses the other of cheating, and a shot
is fired. If the play is read (or heard on radio) we might infer
that the macabre tale is somehow infecting the gamblers,
making them need to act out the same kind of violence as
they hear described. But on stage in Mosher's production,
that was not the case. The importance of story and
storyteller was not as central as implied by the words alone,
but qualified by the evidence of the surrounding scenic
reality. In this production, the story did not influence the
violence which climaxed the game; the card-players were
not even listening to it. The violence in the story and that in
the card game just happened to manifest themselves at the
same time – which in a way made the play even more
disturbing.

But there are many moments in Mamet where a reaction
from a more reticent character is a vital determinant of
whether a scene, or even a whole play, is 'positive' or
'negative' in outcome. Consider the scene in *Sexual
Perversity in Chicago* where Dan attempts to wake Deb. Is
she asleep when he is making his entreaties? Awake and
shamming sleep? Does she wake halfway through? And
what is her reaction before his final line, 'Did I wake you

up?'? Or consider Roma's reaction to Levene's big-sale story in Act II of *Glengarry Glen Ross*. Mamet has stated that he did not intend Roma's approbation of Levene at this point to be qualified by any hint of a snide manipulativeness.[10] But that is not indicated in the script – and a director might well choose to develop a different attitude on Roma's part. Readings of whole plays can depend on this kind of ambiguity – and the solutions that different productions provide. For example, in *Lakeboat* Dale's reaction to Joe's gladness that the missing night cook is returning could help make the play either an upbeat or a downbeat experience for an audience. In *Edmond*, as we have seen, Mosher stressed the positive aspects of Edmond's final moments with the black prisoner, both in the peace and consonance of the dialogue rhythms and the final kiss the men share. In *The Shawl*, a positive colouration was stressed in the final moments between John and Miss A. In *Reunion*, it is not certain from the text alone what kind of effect Bernie is having on Carol – whether she is listening to his ruminative stories reluctantly, coldly, impatiently, or in some other way. Mamet's own production made the play far more 'positive' than it appears on the page. Carol was clearly won over by Bernie's stories, by her father's self-defensiveness, his excuses, his attempts to be open with her. In directing Lindsay Crouse, Mamet told her that during these listening-scenes, 'If the answer is in him, it brings you to life. If it is in you, it brings you to death.'[11]

This kind of ambiguity in Mamet's texts is a positive quality, in spite of the problems it causes directors and critics. The variables which can result from differing interpretations can produce the variation in production which is one of the hallmarks of really rich plays.

American Buffalo has already passed this test. In its brief life it has had a production history which proves just how open to different interpretations it is – and the other major Mamet plays will surely stand up under a variety of directorial readings. According to Mel Gussow, all the significant English-language productions of the play in Chicago, New York, New Haven and London between 1975 and 1983 were distinct in their own ways – and this was especially true of the two productions on Broadway: the Ulu Grosbard production of 1977, and the one by Arvin Brown which originated in New Haven in 1980 and reached Broadway three years later.

Various directorial solutions connected with setting, casting, pacing, subtext interpretation and tonality produced very different overall stagings which were none the less faithful to the text of the play. According to Gussow, the keynote for each production was the actor playing the catalytic role of Teach. Grosbard's production highlighted the incipient threat and violence in the script. Robert Duvall's Teach was a thuggish paranoid struggling to contain, from the very beginning, his urge to lash out. Santo Loquasto's set rendered the junkshop as a dour, threatening symbol of the detritus of capitalism. The violence of the climax of the play was shocking in its impact; the ironic undertone in Teach's litany during this destruction of the junkshop hardly registered. By contrast, Brown's production emphasised the Absurdist-tinged comedy also implicit in much of the play: in static and non-linear elements, the sense of plans going awry, inept actions having inane as well as cruel consequences. This production began its life on the thrust stage of the Long Wharf Theatre – and thus had the effect of scaling the play down and emphasising its propensity, at times, for the intimate, even the casually playful. As portrayed by Al Pacino, Teach appeared lost from the start in a futile dream, and appeared a 'man in distress. He looks dishevelled, a man who has been lying awake nights dreaming about scores and scams.'[12] The junkshop, as designed by Marjorie Bradley Kellogg, seemed more like an offbeat home for the characters than a threatening metaphor for debased capitalism. Lastly, the violence of the climax seemed more like a ritual gesture of defeat, with the irony strongly emphasised, than a passionate lashing-out at the failure of the crime planned and the friendship hoped for. In this production, the play was hailed as a classic American comedy.

The Water Engine illustrates that special elusive 'dimension' which operates when a Mamet play is staged. The play's form and content abound in the dialectical qualities apparent in his work. The text may look minimalist – but in production it proves ground for both fascinating and necessary theatrical expansion. The text's formal framework has great theatrical possibilities, even if on the page it seems strained and schematic. *The Water Engine* is Mamet's most quintessential play as far as content is concerned. It weaves together 'business', with its pressure to abrogate trust; the potential for communion in the mentor–protégé relationship; the tensions caused by sexual pressures.

The central fable of the water engine and its inventor is actually an episode in a radio serial called 'The Century of Progress', which is being broadcast from a radio studio during 1934, the second year of the Chicago World's Fair. Thus a play-within-a-play device operates; and we, the modern audience, are treated as a radio-studio audience in 1934 watching the birth of a fictional creation, privileged to see the trick 'from the back' and be privy to the legerdemain of the radio medium that engenders it. More subtly, we are invited to compare the *Zeitgeist* of our own time with that of the 1930s, without being distracted by obvious parody or camp nostalgia.

The fable itself concerns the aspiration and fate of Charles Lang, a punch-press operator who is also a moonlighting inventor. He builds an engine that will run on water as its only fuel. Lang contacts an attorney, Gross, for a patent. Gross turns him over to one of his cronies, a representative of sinister business interests who wish to buy the invention outright for their own profit. When Lang defies them, they kidnap his sister and hold her to ransom for the plans. Even the police seem to be in league with them. But Lang, moved by an anecdote of a chain letter which insists that 'all people are connected', mails the plans to young Bernie, scientifically talented son of the local storekeeper. Bernie receives the plan; Lang and his sister are found brutally murdered in Waukegan.

The fable walks a fine line between optimism and ironic disillusionment. On the page, disillusionment might seem to prevail, especially when some of the implications of the characterisation are probed. The fable is an illustration of the idea that mankind has been cheated of the altruistic benefits of some marvellous new invention by 'business interests' which have removed them from popular consumption for profit. It illustrates the ruthless destructiveness of 'business' even more directly than *Glengarry Glen Ross* does.

Lang is compromised by the same dream of 'business' success that has undone the Levenes and Teaches of the world. Initially, he and his sister have dreams of being rich and famous because of the engine, and his early intransigence about letting anyone else share the possible profits stems largely from his convictions about personal ownership. His naïveté derives less from moral purity than from egocentricity and childishness, qualities that are also stressed in his relationship with his sister, Rita. Their scenes together form an interesting throwback to the male–female relationships of *Sexual Perversity in Chicago* and *The Woods*, for Rita mothers Charles with a cloying obsessiveness which suggests a maladjusted pair of lovers rather than brother and sister. (In the first Chicago production, Rita was in fact Charles's girlfriend, not his sister.) Lang naïvely believes in the integrity of the 'bargain law' which is supposed to operate in business dealings, and which the play exposes as a sham. Like the characters of *American Buffalo*, Lang cannot distinguish between business and friendship; like the mark Lingk in *Glengarry Glen Ross*, he desperately seeks it in unlikely places. He calls Gross a 'friend' after only one meeting; Gross later refers to his more villainous colleague as a 'friend' after the same fashion, playing on Lang's naïveté to keep him off guard. But Lang has faith in the benefits to humanity of what he has discovered – and this seems to justify to him the laying-down of his own life and his sister's as well. It also seems to him to justify his own dishonesty. He has outfitted his entire laboratory with machinery and equipment 'borrowed' from the firm which employs him. So altruism is inextricably linked with what one of the park speakers calls the 'great dream of avarice' that characterises America.

However, there is much optimism inherent in the play. This aspect of it was stressed in the production by Steven Schachter for Joseph Papp's cabaret format at the Public Theatre in January 1978. Schachter also directed the play at its Chicago premiere for the St Nicholas Theatre the previous year, the version which moved uptown to the Plymouth Theatre in March 1978, and the 1985 revival on the mainstage of the Goodman Theatre.

John Lee Beatty's setting, and Schachter's use of it, made possible an intriguing exercise in social commentary and also in involving the audience. The evening began with a device to remind the audience of its double function, for it was 'cast' as a 1934 radio-studio audience. So all the time the audience was aware that it was privileged – it was asked to applaud on cue, to collaborate with the studio creation of a fictive reality, yet it was also reminded that it was part of a wider audience which, through the radio medium, would be seduced into accepting the fable at a simpler level of make-believe. The naïve complicity asked for by the hearty announcer (Colin Stinton) in introductory material not printed in the text made the audience aware from the outset of the tonal differences between its own and a less disenchanted age. So did Annie Hat's sequence of 1930s standard songs, rendered in historically faithful idiom, which preceded the actual beginning of the 'Water Engine' broadcast. (In the Broadway production, a curtain-raiser, *Mr Happiness*, served the same function, but rather more equivocally.)

By this time, the audience had taken in the implications of the setting which Beatty and Schachter had devised: an interesting compromise between minimalism and something more suggestively poetic. The spartan bareness of the acting-area, with tables and microphones, balanced the 'magic' suggested by the shadowy background details of sound-effects booth and operating-controls. The setting melded the trappings of 1930s radio-studio performance with those of proscenium theatre. The stage was basically arranged like a radio studio, with its upstage section 'glassed off'. There, two silhouetted figures were seen operating dials on two dimly lit consoles, while above them was a clock which showed real time crowned with an 'on air' sign which went red when appropriate. To the right was the sound-effects booth, with a boom microphone to follow various actors as they moved around the studio. A man was inside, as well as several ingenious sound-producing objects sometimes bearing no relation to the objects whose sound they were meant to imitate. The acting-area comprised three levels. Parallel to the audience, a little left of centre on the lowest level, were two long tables, each with two chairs and a table mike on the upstage side. The rest of this level was bare, as were the narrow middle and broader upper ones. They took on place definition in the course of the performance. The upper level served as the elevator area (stage right) and Bernie's father's store (stage left). On the auditorium level, to stage left, sat Alaric Jans at the organ. The use of microphones – the boom, table and standing mikes carried on and off by actors – served to define more indeterminate locations elsewhere. The chain-letter narrations were all done on table mikes in low-angled chiaroscuro. Radio conventions were particularly apparent in incongruities of costume and casting: in dress and physical appearance an actor or actress might be quite unlike the character portrayed.

The setting made for a completely fluid presentation of the play's structure, an easy cross-over between the conventions of radio and theatre. Even the chain-letter narrations, which suggest superstition masquerading as just fate, were organically integrated with the play's other formal devices. What seems on the page to be obtrusive cross-cutting between different times, places and actions was accomplished effortlessly and seamlessly in this production. The conventions gently held in balance the created fable and the artifice behind its construction, and suggested that any conventions of enactment and communication are influenced by the dominant technology of a historical period. Through his chosen manipulation of these conventions, Mamet invites us to ponder the fact that all fables are collusive acts of their time, and that they are all subject to revisitings and revision – and that we may subject contemporary attitudes, and contemporary fables that have grown out of them, to the same kind of scrutiny. This process is similar to what Brecht called 'historification' – the awareness that the present is just another historical period subject to analysis, definition and correction. The difference from Brecht lies in the complete eschewing of political propaganda, in the delight communicated to the audience through the strategy of setting the conventions of enactment in two different media simultaneously.

When we examine how Schachter pointed the text and subtext, we find that it was intimately connected with his orchestration of the battery of sound-effects and music. Of particular significance was the degree to which he foregrounded the radio conventions at any given time, and whether they paralleled or counterpointed the text. Depending on how they were used, the fable itself was authenticated or parodied at certain points, endorsement or irony indicated. The sound-effects included those of the invisible engine, the *religioso* high-reeded organ passages to emphasise Lang's idealism, the throbbing bass notes to stress menace and evil, the 'bled' telephone sound-effects to suggest denatured voices, and the string quartet to suggest Copland-like optimism.

Gradually, the aesthetic outcome of the scenic and directorial strategy became apparent. As the play proceeded, one tended to become more and more involved in the fable, and less aware of the distancing-conventions of its enactment. At the same time, the employment of semaphoric musical or sound-effects, and the ingenious use of space to suggest alienation, decreased. By the end of Act I the fleshing-out and pointing-up of the subtext, especially in terms of realisation and epiphany, had come into its own as an effective method of focusing overall significance, and the effects of this continued to be felt through most of Act II. The most important such moment was the climax, Lang's realisation that all people are connected. At times of real import, when a timeless truth breaks through the static of period detail and media conventions, Schachter presented the moment 'straight' – no sound-effects, no music, no movement:

> VOICE OVER *stops. They stop.* BARKER *reads:*
> 'Who knows the real power of man's soul?'
> 'Much good, much pain and misery is caused by our beliefs.
> Great Wealth and Fame stand just beyond your grasp.
> All civilization stands on trust.
> All people are connected.
> No man can call back what one man does.'
> LANG. What?
> BARKER. I'm sorry?
> LANG. Would you read that part again?
> *Pause.*
> BARKER. Sure.
> *Pause.*
> 'All people are connected.'
> LANG. Yes, yes.
> BARKER. 'No man can call back what one man does.'

The force invested in this moment through the simple presentation was carried over into the following reversal. As the lawyer threatens Lang for the last time, the Speaker on Bughouse Hill presents a vision of apocalypse as America 'commences the fulfilment of its malevolent destiny as The New World'. The Moderator, clearly hoping for a rebuttal, pleads, 'Anybody want to speak? Does anybody want to speak?', but there is silence after each question, and this suggests a void of moral impotence as chilling as that which descends in *American Buffalo* after Teach's cry on destroying the shop that 'There is nothing out there.'

Schachter swung the play away from darkness in the final moments. The entering mailman gave letters to the father, and the letters were mimed. Then he turned to Bernie and said, 'And it seems I've got one for *you*', and the letter with the plans inside was real. In the text of the play, there are final lines that qualify the optimism of this moment, that imply that the plans will not survive, that 'in torn and filthy manuscripts misfiled in secondhand bookstores, here rest the vestiges of this and other cultures. Arcane Knowledge in transition from the inaccessible to the occult, as we rush on.' We know this to be true. But Schachter provided a gentle counterpoint with consolatory violin music by Alaric Jans. The music also neutralised the import of the following chain-letter voice, with its uneasy equation of human interconnectedness and superstitious chicanery. Bernie continues to stare at the plans, and he finally reads them. The Barker announces that the fair is closing for the day, and that the tickets people hold are good for tomorrow.

At the end, the audience was reminded of its two roles as 1934 and modern audience, and of the difference between the two eras. The effect was to create uneasiness. The 1934 audience was wished a warm goodnight by the Announcer, in the same saccharine, reassuring voice of the play's beginning. That fiction was in turn exploded, and the spectators were recast as a contemporary audience when the actors came out and took a conventional curtain call. This abrogated the time warp. Mamet, aided by his fine director, had sustained a Bettelheim-like fable in the theatre, and at the same time had exposed some of its built-in evasions and inconsistencies.

In most of Mamet's plays there is a struggle between a positive drive to contact and negative movement to isolation fostered by the destructive 'business' spirit; but, when the plays are staged, the former is accentuated. In Mamet's theory of acting, the basis of his preferred technique rests on actors playing 'the moment' and reacting truthfully to the stimulus from other actors. It is perhaps axiomatic that, in any production of any play, the physical presence of the actors will tend to emphasise the communicative aspect, as actors in performance play off and react to each other – and even the nuances of a determination *not* to communicate involve a display of teamwork. This is part of that extra dimension that Beatty recognises in Mamet's plays when they are staged in the theatre.

8
Mamet in Context

In an introductory study on Mamet, it is inevitable that the major plays should receive the primary focus. Mamet's is, however, a many-sided artistic talent, and it is time to round out the picture with a brief consideration of his other work. There are essays and occasional articles, adaptations of plays by other playwrights, children's plays and work in progress. Most important, there are some characteristic short plays and sketches that seem fated to comparative theatrical neglect, both because of their brevity and because of the demands they sometimes make on audiences. We must also consider Mamet's place in the larger context of drama and theatre, though at this stage in his career, we can reach only a provisional assessment.

A collection of Mamet's essays, *Writing in Restaurants*, throws valuable light on his intentions in certain specific plays and on his work as a whole. Often the essays relate to the larger question of the malaise in society; a reiterated theme is Americans' preoccupation with the faddish and the inauthentic. Many of the essays reveal an overt didacticism that is stimulating, but fortunately absent from the plays themselves.

Among Mamet's adaptations of plays by others, those of Pierre Laville's *Le Fleuve rouge* (*Red River*, 1983) and Chekhov's *The Cherry Orchard* (1985) are fairly faithful to the structure and themes of the original plays but, in the case of the Chekhov, less so to the tone and the letter. Mamet's version of *The Cherry Orchard* changes the predominantly *legato* style of older translations and adaptations such as those of David Magarshack and Stark Young. What is often considered 'period' fidelity to tone and mood is rejected for more contemporary resonances. Dialogue is broken down into terse sentences and astringent rhythms, and there are the characteristic Mamet thumbprints of syntactic dislocations, repetitions, elision of connectives, sputterings, and collapses into pauses and silence. The niceties of social distinction in the original also tend to be eroded, but Mamet sees the play as being less about opposing class outlooks than about unfulfilled sexuality.[1] His version of the play is arresting – but, in the process of removing some of the old varnish from a masterwork, he may have removed some of the paint as well.

His three children's plays are all refreshingly free of the innocuous, patronising fustian often associated with such plays; indeed the plays are as suitable for parents as for children. They all have quite complicated narratives, and all have morals as good fables should. The first two present ample opportunities for exuberant, farcical staging.

The Poet and the Rent is a playful allegory about the artist in society. A poet named David has a series of pittoresque adventures as he strives to get $60 to pay his rent. After turning down a $40,000-a-year job in an advertising-

agency, he is rewarded in the end by getting his rent paid
for two years so that he can write.

*The Revenge of the Space Pandas, or, Binky Rudich and
the Two-Speed Clock* gently satirises television shows such
as *Star Trek*. The hero, his girl playmate and a dirty sheep
called Bob are transported to a planet fifty light-years away
from earth by a two-speed clock they invent. The clock
operates on 'real' time and something similar to
'durational' time, so it is a vehicle to escape mundanity and
for travel into the realm of something more exciting. The
planet, called Crestview because the inhabitants 'thought it
might attract investors', proves to be inhabited by giant
pandas, two of whom are called Buffy and Boots, and a
tyrant called George Topax, who wants to detain Bob so he
can get a football sweater. An old matinee idol called Ed
Farpis saves the trio from execution by pumpkin guillotine;
the two-speed clock is repaired with a paper clip; and the
three come home to Waukegan in time for a casserole lunch
they earlier despised.

The Frog Prince is an altogether darker piece, much
more spare and restrained in language, plot and staging. A
prince is picking flowers in a field for his betrothed. A
peasant woman who owns the field asks for the flowers and
is refused, whereupon the prince is changed into a frog. To
become human again, the prince must be kissed in unselfish
love by someone who does not know his story. Eventually
this happens – but not before his faithful servant has lost his
life looking after him. Then he picks flowers again – this
time for his friend's grave. Again, the peasant woman asks
for the flowers. Again, he is about to refuse – but thinks
better of it, puts his ego aside, and gives them to her. *The
Frog Prince*, more so than the earlier children's plays,
incorporates motifs from the adult ones, notably the idea of

the 'hag' which must be exposed, and the Campbell mythic pattern of departure, initiation and return.

The short plays, sketches and monologues constitute some of Mamet's most demanding and 'experimental' dramatic writing. They do not, however, exemplify what Mamet has disparagingly called 'esthetic politics'; they all have something to say – though precisely what has sometimes baffled audiences, even actors. If the children's plays have an affinity with some of the more communion-centred longer plays, these shorter pieces reinforce Mamet's connection with the Pinter–Beckett tradition, even when they deal with specifically American characters and locales. They are coloured with the dark side of Mamet's world, and the most interesting of the pieces formally embody a sense of dislocation and discontinuity. The recently published *Goldberg Street* (1985) reprints all the material contained in the earlier collection *Short Plays and Monologues* except for *Prairie du Chien*, and it contains some more recent pieces.

The most memorable of these short works alienate the standard processes of verbal and theatrical communication. They go beyond Beckett and Pinter's concerns and enter the territory of playwrights such as Peter Handke and Heiner Müller, for they foreground the conventions by which words stand for objects and concepts. *Litko*, an early monologue performed with *The Duck Variations* at the Body Politic in 1972, is like a playful Handke *Sprechstück*. Mamet calls into question all the conventions of 'effective' theatre, realistic or otherwise, as perceived by an audience in a 'normal' theatre evening. *The Spanish Prisoner* (1985) is a brief but dense set of two variations on the theme of the will to exploit. The first of these focuses on the image of a Spanish galleon which disappeared in a hurricane, laden with treasure from an exploited subject people; the second, on the death of a promising black youth. In Chicago, Mosher staged this short play as a prelude to *The Shawl* – a play which deals with transcendence over the will to exploit. He also gave the play a more realistic framework in performance than appears on the page, where the four speakers are differentiated by capital letters only. They talk in indigestible and convoluted middle-class thickets of verbiage; but one of them proposes the idea that the will to exploit developed out of a world where rationality is valued over passion. In *Yes*, two men gradually sputter into silence when they examine some of the clichés of affection and regard. This play finishes with a total linguistic breakdown similar to that in *Edmond* where the hero cannot tell the Chaplain why he has killed. Here the breakdown is even more unnerving because its apparent cause is so trivial.

Crosspatch (1985), a short play first performed with its more conventional companion piece *Goldberg Street* on radio, also highlights difficulties in communication, as a group of legionnaires meet at a convention. The play is interesting and atypical for Mamet in that it uses much direct address to the audience; the audience is 'cast' by implication as other legionnaires in the convention hall, and the play could be staged with 'plants' in the theatre to emphasise this. It ends with a fascistic litany that implicates the audience in the values expressed. Before this, three speakers take the stand and make long speeches in which linear logic has been corroded by liquor. For all their obscurities, these speeches delineate a shared regret for the passing of a 'quality' of life which made it easier to fight and kill with a clear conscience. In *Goldberg Street*, that earlier time is more positively evoked when a father tells his young daughter of his war service and how the erosion of his Jewish identity was subsumed in a sense of communion with mankind as he wept with war survivors at the Normandy reunion.

Many of the other short plays and monologues also treat themes of failure to connect, dislocation and disillusionment – but more within the parameters of standard realism, with less emphasis on phenomenological disjunctions. In *Yes But So What*, two men sit and ponder the possible connection between inner motives and happenstance in the outer world, but come to no conclusions about it. In *Food*, another two desperately try to form a connection between types of food and greater longevity, but fail.

A more extended focus on the same theme is provided by *The Disappearance of the Jews*, staged in 1983 but still not published, which is a darker-hued *Reunion*. Set in a Chicago hotel room, the play concerns a meeting after some years of two old school friends in their late thirties: Joey, a restaurateur, and Bobby, who is briefly visiting from the south. The play consists entirely of conversations which expose the fact that intimacy, if it ever existed, is irrecoverable. The encounter begins with reminiscences about old girlfriends, but the details are blurred. Both men are disappointed with their marriages, one of which has broken up. As they try to find a connection to their Jewish heritage, they examine the roots of that tradition, in both Europe and America, but find little tangible to give them a sense of meaning. Joey laments that '*every* thing is so far from us this day. And we have no connection . . . .'[2] Later, he says that he believes there are societies where people have found purpose through ritual, ceremony and prayer; but, as far as he is concerned, 'I think I invent *ceremonies*, but I never keep them up.' He confesses that he and his wife have just joined a synagogue; but it is new. Its lack of efficacy is implied:

> BOBBY. What do you do, you *go* there . . .
> JOEY.   . . . we just joined . . .
> BOBBY. You *did*.
> JOEY. Yeah. (*Pause.*)

Then the topic of old girlfriends is recycled. At the end, Joey wants cigarettes, but not enough to go and get them; he asks Bobby whether he wants them enough to go, but Bobby replies, 'I almost do, but I shouldn't.' Here the characters' will to contact is weaker than in any other Mamet play – and one of the playwright's bleakest, most Beckett-like visions trails into silence.

The sketches grouped under umbrella titles, notably *The Blue Hour* and *Vermont Sketches*, dilute this evocation of a personal void with a stronger sense of socio-political reality. The second of the *Vermont Sketches*, 'Pint's a Pound the World Round', deals with the difficulty of small independent businesses surviving in the face of competition from more ruthless and impersonal cartels. The powerful opening segment of *The Blue Hour* is a scabrous encounter between doctor and patient, in which she accuses him of exploiting and overcharging her. *In Old Vermont* astutely combines a sense of metaphysical dread with a social statement. It is a dialogue between a man and woman in a secure, modern Vermont farm; but the complacency of the present falls away as a past horror invades the cosy interior. The woman has a vision of an Indian massacre, with hacked genitals and roasted flesh, a violent retaliation for exploitation and expropriation. We are reminded of Nick's climactic nightmare bear story in *The Woods*.

There are two main lines of influence or comparison which go some way to explain the appeal of Mamet's work to both American and international audiences. The former relates to the mainline American 'realist' dramatic tradition, with its greater socio-political emphasis; the latter relates to the Pinter–Beckett tradition of entropic menace, discontinuity and mystery, with metaphysical overtones. Mamet himself acknowledges influence from the second source. He admits that Pinter impressed him in his early reading, through works such as *The Homecoming*, *The Basement* (1967, interestingly a film script) and the revue sketches. He told Mel Gussow that 'I felt a huge freedom because of Pinter's sketches – to deal in depth and on their own merit with such minutiae. Beckett and Pinter – of course I'm influenced by them. If you're in modern dance, how could you not be influenced by Martha Graham?'[3] He also acted in *The Homecoming*, and in 1983 Pinter was a great help to Mamet in setting up the premiere of *Glengarry Glen Ross*.

But Mamet's chief context as playwright and man of the theatre has been the American one – and it is in the context of American drama and theatre that he can be most illuminatingly placed. At high school and Hull House, there were the contacts with the work of Kenneth Brown, Tad Mosel, Murray Schisgal and various musicals; at Second City, the improvised comedy influenced by Sills, Spolin and the skit structure. And Mamet soon became aware of the American literary and dramatic socio-realist tradition, and early on admitted his desire to write this kind of play.[4] He has compared *Reunion* to the first act of *Anna Christie* by O'Neill; *Lakeboat* has affiliations with the same playwright's short 'sea' plays; he has adapted and directed *Beyond the Horizon*; he has described Act II of *Glengarry Glen Ross* as a 'kind of homage to Sidney Kingsley'.[5] Mamet has mentioned at different times specific influences from American literature and drama: Hemingway (by far the most frequently cited influence from American sources, as Pinter has been from European), Dreiser, Mencken and the Chicago playwright Wallace Shawn.

Possibly the greatest influences from the American realist tradition are those not of play or fiction-writing, but of acting and staging. Techniques of fixing a play's 'superobjective', dividing a play into a 'through line' of 'beats', defining the dominant action of each 'beat', and playing such actions clearly but responding each night on stage in and for the 'moment' – all this constitutes a mainstay of the American realistic performance tradition, and consequently has had a seminal effect on the form and style of most plays written to be performed in the American theatre. While the techniques can be traced back to Stanislavsky and his first-generation pupils, they owe more to the 'fervent years' of the 1930s and the Group Theatre.

When Mamet began his career in the early 1970s, this tradition was under heavy fire. The Living and Open Theatres, Performance Group and other ensembles had developed a surreal theatre based on abrogation of plot, character and realistic dialogue, in which Artaudian theory and Grotowskian practice were more prominent. When realism regained ground in the mid 1970s, it was not quite the transparent realism of old. The pervasive conventions of the old 'well-made' play – linear plot, fully inflected characterisation, and dialogue delimited by its traditional purpose to further both these – suffered a sea change. Plots were more often based on indirect action or stasis; characters could often not explain their motives and were unsure of their own histories; dialogue frequently functioned as an independent poetry divorced from plot and character development. Realism was now far more self-reflexive, indelibly coloured with Absurdism from the

European tradition of Beckett and Pinter. It has been called 'new realism' (Richard Eder), and 'renovated realism' (Christopher Bigsby),[6] to trot out just two serviceable labels; and its emergence inevitably affected the direction and audience perception of Mamet's work, as it did that of many of his fellow playwrights.

The first Mamet plays to appear were sometimes related to the work of playwrights prominent in a slightly earlier period – playwrights such as Jean Claude van Itallie and Megan Terry, who especially dealt with the stereotypification of social role-playing and its per-vasiveness in American life. Their reliance on social caricature as a device is also apparent in some of the first Mamet plays to garner critical attention. Gradually, the underpinnings of these techniques in a distinctively orchestrated, spare realism became more apparent.

The same kind of development is also noticeable in the work of some of Mamet's peer playwrights. Consideration of the careers of some of them during the same period helps to point to similarities with Mamet, and it also helps to underline the ways in which his work was individual.

Many American playwrights whom critics had earlier thought Absurdist or surreal shifted their strategy from about 1975 on, so that the 'new realism' more palpably emerged. For example, Lanford Wilson resurrected the 'well-made' play and foregrounded motifs of earlier realism in an almost self-reflexive manner in plays such as *The Fifth of July* (1978) and *Talley's Folly* (1979). This superseded the open structure and surreal elements of several plays of the 1960s, such as *The Rimers of Eldritch* (1966) and *Balm in Gilead* (1965). John Guare continued to write plays in which black comedy was paramount, but his path from *Muzeeka* (1968) and *Cop-Out* (1969) to *Bosoms and Neglect* (1979) was marked by increased restraint in using surrealism and presentational devices. The scabrous satire of Christopher Durang traversed a path from the comfortably ridiculous *The Nature and Purpose of the Universe* (1971) to *Sister Mary Ignatius Explains It All for You* (1979), a play uncomfortably closer to realism. Emergent playwrights such as Albert Innaurato, Michael Cristofer, Beth Henley and Marsha Norman relied heavily on the 'new' realism. Even a bright and more individual talent such as Wallace Shawn used the basic realism of a Shavian 'discussion' play to brilliant effect, lacing it with surrealism, but firmly centring the thrust of his plays in the argumentation of dialogue. Shawn's use of dialogue as a major dramaturgical element brings his work close to Mamet's in some respects. But the cases of Sam Shepard and David Rabe warrant closer attention for the way their own development in these years can be compared and contrasted with Mamet's.

Shepard still uses verbal 'arias' as major metaphors for his characters' states of mind, and many such 'arias' register as surreal and presentational set pieces, even though they now tend to occur within a more realistic context than was apparent in his work before 1975. Like Mamet's, Shepard's use of words is often not much related to traditional dramatic plot – there is no way so to justify long solo speeches such as those of Halie in Act I of *Buried Child* (1978) or of Wesley in Act I of *Curse of the Starving Class* (1976). Shepard differs from Mamet, however, in that, even when such extended speeches incorporate elements of defensiveness and social mask, they are also windows onto the imaginative landscape of characters' minds. They are not stories told to others; they are reproductions of thought-processes. Since the dialogue of such passages is mostly interiorised, it is not constructed on the rhythms of spoken language as used in 'reality'. And the dialogue of

Shepard's plays tends to be more lyrical and imagistic than Mamet's. Thus, though both playwrights place much emphasis on language in the dramaturgical hierarchy, purpose and effect are different.

The career of Rabe, especially his use of language, provides a closer parallel with Mamet. The surrealism and fractured structures of *The Basic Training of Pavlo Hummel* (1968) and *Sticks and Bones* (1969) have evolved into the more conventional structures and observance of the unities apparent in *Streamers* (1976) and *Hurlyburly* (1983). Especially in the latter play, language is a source from which the characters seek the reassurance of an identity they can act out, a shore against a void of silence they dare not confront. The characters of *Hurlyburly* are more articulate, their words more in tandem with their conscious purpose, than Mamet's. But, as Rabe says in his stage directions, '*in the characters' speeches phrases such as "whatchamacallit", "thingamajig", "blah-blah-blah" and "rapateta" abound. These are phrases used by the characters to keep themselves talking and should be said unhesitatingly with the authority and conviction with which one would have in fact said the missing word.*'[7] The characters keep themselves talking for the same reason that so many of Mamet's do. Their reliance on easily accessible language is role-playing – for reassurance, for deflection, for one-upmanship, for acting out an identity mask which keeps the vulnerable part of themselves hidden and not even fully realised to themselves. Rabe's characters, for the most part, are aware of what they are doing; Mamet's are often not. A character in Christopher Durang's *Titanic* (1974) says, 'Sometimes when I don't make connections between statements, I worry. And sometimes . . . I don't care.'[8] A similar attitude often inhabits characters in the more 'negative' Mamet plays and elicits moral dismay from the

audience. Rabe's characters' greater awareness is evidence
of a more consciously didactic moral attitude on the
playwright's part, and elicits a more conventionally
sympathetic response from the audience.

Critics have said that what separates Mamet from his
peers, what gives him his signature style and his
individuality, is his dialogue. The dialogue is indeed
individual and unmistakable, and can hardly be confused
with that of any other playwright – and that irrespective of
whether it is grounded in the Chicago street (*American
Buffalo*) or the middle-class parlour (*The Shawl*). It led
some critics to put too little emphasis on its connection to
themes, situation and characterisation; and it led some to
argue that some plays were talk-centred by default rather
than design. But the dialogue is the chief vehicle of the
dialectical principle in Mamet: the disjunctions between
the overt meanings of the words and the implied meanings
of their rhythms; between the ebullience of the speaker and
the reactions of the listener; or between the speaker and his
words and the silences he wants to cover and deny. These
silences at times embody threat, at other times the
possibility of contact.

Mamet has built an international reputation, in spite of
the difficulties of rendering his unique dialogue in
translation, or even filtering it through the mouths of
non-American actors. Since 1981, there have been
productions of *The Woods* in Israel, Germany,
Switzerland, Austria, Belgium and Holland, and there
have been English-language productions in South Africa
and Australia. *All Men are Whores: An Inquiry* was done in
Vienna by the English Theatre in 1985. *The Water Engine*
was performed on German television and radio during
1984–5. *Prairie du Chien* has been given three times on

German radio since 1979. *Reunion* has been broadcast on Finnish radio, and *Edmond* on Danish and Swedish radio. *Edmond* was also produced on stage in England at the Royal Court Theatre and the Newcastle Playhouse in 1985. And by early 1986 *Glengarry Glen Ross* had been seen in London, Dublin, Melbourne, Perth, Cape Town, Johannesburg, Pretoria, Edmonton, Marseille, Tokyo, Milan, Tel Aviv, Copenhagen, and in various productions in Germany, Switzerland, Austria, Holland and Belgium. It has also been heard on Swedish radio.[9] Obviously the conclusion to be drawn from this is that Mamet's plays do translate, and for non-English-speaking audiences Mamet's plays obviously mean a great deal despite the loss of Mametspeak in its original form.

What, then, are other points of his distinctiveness? Christopher Bigsby, in his stimulating work on Mamet, stresses the playwright's affinity to the European Absurdist tradition of Beckett and Pinter, though he also draws attention to the affiliation with the American realist tradition. Bigsby's reading of Mamet sharpens Mamet's individual profile and explains his international appeal. He is the American playwright who most boldly refuses easy consolation and sentimental reassurance to his audience and, through his techniques of minimalism and discontinuity, creates a world where 'entropy rules'. Bigsby acknowledges that 'for the most part his plays seem to end reassuringly', but the 'simple gesture of consolation or shared experience is simply not powerful enough to neutralise the fears, the incompletions and the isolation exposed by the motion of the play'.[10] The possibility of genuine communion is only acknowledged by the playwright in his creation of the plays themselves, as bulwarks against the incipient meaninglessness of life, and by the fact that Mamet believes in the communion between artists and audience in the theatre. 'Like Albee,' Bigsby writes,

> Mamet is a poet of loss. The world he creates is one drained of transcendence, one in which individuals no longer communicate because they share nothing but their situation. They are role-players deprived of an audience, entropic figures struggling to come to terms with their own depleting energy.[11]

This reading is too reductive. Certain plays do not fit it at all easily; it underemphasises the effect of certain plays as they unfold in the time–space continuum of performance; and it denies Mamet's work the variety that is its due.

Mamet is a Chicago writer, and can be considered part of the vigorous Chicago literary tradition. He believes that his predecessors all finally wrote the same story, 'a story of possibility, because the idea in the air is that the West is beginning, and that life is capable of being both understood and enjoyed.'[12]

The more one examines Mamet's world, the more one is struck by its energy. While Mamet's characters are hobbled by their inability to free themselves from hand-me-down societal maxims which have wrongly directed their energies, some of them do surmount the masks which society has imposed on them. They struggle through pressures towards competition and one-upmanship to achieve relationships in which loyalty can operate. They struggle to become more than items in sexual commodity exchange to each other. Or, alone, they strive, like the protagonist in *Edmond*, to make a clearing-house for their true natures in a situation where professional and social obligations have straitjacketed them. Even when pursuing the wrong goals, they strive mightily to reach them, and not only through language. Mamet cautiously lets us celebrate their tentative success in getting together, with an avoidance of sentiment. And especially in production, through the underlying rhythm of the sometimes bald-looking words, he drives home his characters' powerful will to make contact with one another.

Mamet's importance, apart from the dialogue, lies in his unsentimental sense of personal and social morality, his wry but sharp sense of dialectic, and the vigour of his characters' intent. The plays reveal a richness under the spareness, a variety of perspectives, a traditional realism of Chekhovian density. This is not to say that Mamet writes the sort of plays that any earlier American realist could have written; his are indelibly coloured in rhythm, structure and tone with the anxieties and disenchantments of post-Vietnam America. Each major play has the potential for many differing interpretations and productions. This is the mark of any major artist whose special qualities nag at the sensibilities, but who cannot be too easily pigeonholed or defined. His achievements already stamp him as a major American playwright of his generation, whose work has both the vividness and the power to cross national boundaries.

References

1. Mid-Career

1. Mel Gussow, 'Stage: Two Pungent Comedies by New Playwright' (review of *Sexual Perversity in Chicago* and *The Duck Variations*), *New York Times*, 1 November 1975, p. 15.

2. Richard Christiansen, 'The Young Lion of Chicago Theater', *Chicago Tribune Magazine*, 11 July 1982, p. 12.

3. Ibid., p. 10.

4. Unless otherwise specified, direct quotations from and biographical information about Mamet in this chapter are taken from a personal interview with the playwright in New York on 9 January 1986.

5. Quoted by Samuel G. Freedman, 'The Gritty Eloquence of David Mamet', *New York Times Magazine*, 21 April 1985, p. 46.

6. Interviewed in *Sanford Meisner: The Theater's Best Kept Secret*, Playhouse Repertory, New York, 1984 (videocassette in the TOFT Collection, Billy Rose Theatre Collection, New York Public Library, Lincoln Center).

7. G. Gerald Fraser, 'David Mamet (on his Career)', *New York Times*, 5 July 1976, section 7, p. 1.

8. Transcription of WFMT broadcast (typescript in Goodman Theatre Archives, Chicago Public Library, Special Collections Division).

9. Unless otherwise specified, statistics for openings and lengths of run are taken from reviews published on individual productions or from the *Best Plays* series of theatre yearbooks, ed. Otis L. Guernsey Jr (New York: Dodd, Mead and Company).

10. See Ned Chaillet's review '*Sexual Perversity in Chicago/Duck Variations*', in *The Times*, 2 December 1977, p. 9; and Peter Stothard's in *Plays and Players*, February 1978, p. 30.

11. Samuel G. Freedman, '*Glengarry* is Helped by Pulitzer', *New York Times*, 24 April 1984, p. C15. Production statistics prepared by John Gersten, Rosenstone/Wender.

2. 'A Sense of Moral Dismay'

1. Mel Gussow, 'The Daring Visions of Four New, Young Playwrights', *New York Times*, 13 February 1977, section 2, p. 9.

2. David Mamet, 'First Principles' (typescript), p. 1.

3. Quoted in *Contemporary Authors*, ed. Frances Carol Locher, 81–4 (Detroit: Gale Research Company, 1979) p. 353.

4. Mamet, 'Decadence' (typescript) pp. 1–2.

5. Peter Weiss, *Marat/Sade*, English version by Geoffrey Skelton, verse adaptation by Adrian Mitchell (London: John Calder, 1965) p. 35 (Act I).

6. Quoted in Marilynn Preston, 'The Dream Rises to Top in Mamet Theory', *Chicago Tribune*, 16 November 1977, section 2, p. 4.

7. C. W. E. Bigsby, *David Mamet*, Contemporary Writers Series (London: Methuen, 1985) pp. 50–1, 74–7.

8. Quoted by Hillary DeVries, 'In David Mamet's Hands a Pen Becomes a Whip', *Christian Science Monitor*, 21 March 1984, p. 22.

9. Clifford Terry, 'At Work and Plays with David Mamet', *Chicago Tribune*, 8 May 1977, section 9, p. 6.

10. Ross Wetzsteon, 'David Mamet: Remember That Name', *Village Voice*, 5 July 1976, pp. 101–4.

11. See Michael VerMeulen, 'The Language of Mamet', *Chicagoland*, 3 June 1977, p. 20; and Robert Storey, 'The Making of David Mamet', *Hollins Critic*, 16, no. 4 (October 1979) p. 3.

12. Mamet, 'Semantic Chickens' (typescript), pp. 2–5.

13. Bigsby, *Mamet*, pp. 61–2.

14. Bruno Bettelheim, *The Uses Of Enchantment: The Meaning and Importance Of Fairy Tales* (New York: Alfred A. Knopf, 1976) pp. 12–19, 29–37, 116–18.

15. Mamet, 'A National Dream Life', *Dramatists' Guild Quarterly*, 15, no. 3 (Autumn 1978) p. 32.

16. Mamet, 'Radio Drama' (typescript), pp. 3–5.

17. Robert Brustein, 'On Theater: Show and Tell', *New Republic*, 7 May 1984, p. 29.

3. Business: 'American Buffalo' (1975); 'Glengarry Glen Ross' (1983)

1. Mel Gussow, 'Real Estate World a Model for Mamet: His New Play Draws on Life', *New York Times*, 28 March 1984, p. C19.

2. Thorstein Veblen, *The Theory of the Leisure Class: An Economic Study of Institutions* (1899; New York: Modern Library, 1934) pp. 236–8.

3. Quoted in William A. Raidy, 'Will Success Buffalo David Mamet? Are You Kidding?', *Chicago Daily News*, 2–3 April 1977 (clipping in Goodman Theatre Archives, Chicago Public Library, Special Collections Division).

4. Quoted in Bigsby. *Mamet*, p. 111.

5. Harold Clurman, 'Theater', *Nation*, 224 (1977) p. 313.

6. Bigsby, *Mamet*, pp. 79–82.

7. Steve Lawson, 'Language Equals Action', *Horizon*, November 1977, p. 43.

8. Stanley Kauffman, 'American Past and Present', *Saturday Review*, 10, no. 39 (1984) p. 59.

9. David Denby, 'Stranger in a Strange Land: A Moviegoer at the Theatre', *Atlantic Monthly*, 255, no. 1 (1985) p. 48.

10. Michael Billington, 'Mamet Turns to the World of Salesmen', *New York Times*, 9 October 1983, section 2, p. 6.

11. Bigsby, p. 122.

12. Quoted in Richard Gottlieb, 'The Engine that Drives Playwright David Mamet', *New York Times*, 15 January 1978, section 2, p. 1.

4. Sex: 'Sexual Perversity in Chicago' (1974); 'The Woods' (1977)

1. Gussow, 'The Daring Visions of Four New, Young Playwrights', *New York Times*, 13 February 1977, section 2, p. 13.

2. Terry Curtis Fox and Eileen Blumenthal disagreed on the merits of *The Woods* in a composite review by three different critics, 'Mamet à trois', *Village Voice*, 7 May 1979, p. 103.

3. Bigsby, *Mamet*, pp. 46–7.

4. Richard Eder, 'Stage: Mamet's *Perversity*. Mosaic on Modern Mores, Moves' (review of *Sexual Perversity in Chicago* and *The Duck Variations*), *New York Times*, 17 June 1976, p. 29.

5. Ibid., p. 29.

6. Bigsby, *Mamet*, pp. 22–4.

7. Mamet, *All Men are Whores: An Inquiry*, in *Goldberg Street: Short Plays And Monologues* (New York: Grove Press, 1985) p. 199.

5. Learning: 'The Duck Variations' (1972); 'Squirrels' (1974); 'A Life in the Theatre' (1977); 'Lakeboat' (1980)

1. Mamet, 'A Tradition of the Theater as Art' (manuscript), p. 1.
2. Bigsby, *Mamet*, pp. 30–1.
3. In interview with Richard Barr, *Emerging Playwrights*, 1977 (videocassette in the TOFT Collection, Billy Rose Theatre Collection, New York Public Library, Lincoln Center).
4. Mamet, *The Duck Variations*, in *'Sexual Perversity in Chicago' and 'The Duck Variations'* (New York: Grove Press, 1978) p. 73.
5. Quoted in Bigsby, *Mamet*, p. 26.
6. Steven H. Gale, 'David Mamet: The Plays, 1972–1980', in *Essays on Contemporary American Drama*, ed. Hedwig Bock and Albert Wertheim (Munich: Max Hueber, 1981) p. 208.
7. Richard Christiansen, *'Squirrels* Play is Extraordinary' (review of *Squirrels*), *Chicago Daily News*, 11 October 1974 (clipping in St Nicholas Theatre Archives, Chicago Public Library, Special Collections Division).
8. Interview with the author.
9. Interview with the author.
10. Interview with the author.
11. 'The World of the Lakeboat', Goodman Theatre Study Guide to *Lakeboat*, ed. Stephen B. Scott (Chicago: Goodman Theatre, 1982) pp. 5, 11–12.

6. Communion: 'The Verdict' (1982); 'Edmond' (1982); 'Lone Canoe, or, The Explorer' (1979); 'Dark Pony' (1977); 'Reunion' (1976); 'The Shawl' (1985)

1. Mamet, *The Verdict*, final draft of screenplay, 23 November 1981, p. 48. I am grateful to Mr David Brown of Zanuck/Brown for making the screenplay available, and to Twentieth Century Fox Film Corporation for permission to quote.
2. Robert Sklar, *Cineaste*, 12, no. 4 (1983) p. 47; repr. in *Film Review Annual 1983*, ed. Jerome S. Ozer (Englewood, NJ: Film Review Publications, 1984) p. 1283.
3. Quoted in Trevor Thomas, 'His Words Get under the Skin', *Los Angeles Times*, 17 June 1984, Calendar section, p. 40.
4. Interview with the author.
5. Joseph Campbell, *The Hero with a Thousand Faces*, Bollingen Series, 17 (Princeton, NJ: Princeton University Press, 1949) pp. 105, 162.
6. Bigsby, *Mamet*, pp. 105–7.

7. Robert Brustein, 'On Theater: The Shape of the New', *New Republic*, 5 July 1982, p. 24.

8. Campbell, *The Hero with a Thousand Faces*, pp. 190–1.

9. *Reunion*, directed by Lamont Johnson, a Lion's Gate Production in association with ABS Video Enterprises, 1982 (videocassette in the TOFT Collection, Billy Rose Theatre Collection, New York Public Library, Lincoln Center).

10. Quoted in Freedman, 'The Gritty Eloquence of David Mamet', *New York Times Magazine*, 21 April 1985, p. 64.

7. The Plays in the Theatre: 'The Water Engine' (1977)

1. Quoted by Richard Christiansen, 'Designing Sets Well with Beatty', *Chicago Tribune*, 15 June 1979, section 3, p. 10.

2. Interview with the author.

3. Interview with the author.

4. Mamet, 'Radio Drama' (typescript), p. 7.

5. Mamet, 'Realism' (manuscript), p. 1.

6. Particularly by Frank Rich. See, for example, 'Theater: A Mamet Play. *Glengarry Glen Ross*' (review, *New York Times*, 26 March, 1984, p. C17.

7. All production details cited in this chapter, other than those for *Prairie du Chien* and *The Shawl*, which were seen live at the Lincoln Center Theatre, derive from videotapes in the TOFT Collection. See Bibliography for a list of the TOFT tapes.

8. Meredith Anthony, 'Nuts over *Squirrels*' (review), *Chicago Reader*, 18 October 1974, p. 15.

9. Interview with the author.

10. Interview with the author.

11. Mamet in 'The Playwright Directs', WNET *Camera Three* (videocassette in the TOFT Collection, Billy Rose Theatre Collection, New York Public Library, Lincoln Center).

12. Mel Gussow, 'Al Pacino Takes on *American Buffalo*,' *New York Times*, 26 October 1980, section 2, p. 3.

8. Mamet in Context

1. Mamet, 'Notes on *The Cherry Orchard*', (typescript), pp. 5–10.

2. Mamet, *The Disappearance of the Jews* (typescript), p. 121. I am

grateful to David Mamet and Rosenstone/Wender for making the typescript available.

3. Quoted in Gussow, 'The Daring Visions of Four New, Young Playwrights', *New York Times*, 13 February 1977, section 2, p. 13.

4. Fraser, 'David Mamet (on his Career)', *New York Times*, 5 July 1976, section 7, p. 1.

5. Quoted in Jennifer Allen, 'David Mamet's Hard Sell', *New York*, 9 April 1984, p. 40.

6. See Richard Eder, 'David Mamet's New Realism', *New York Times Magazine*, 12 March 1978, pp. 40–3; and C. W. E. Bigsby, *A Critical Introduction to Twentieth Century American Drama*, III: *Beyond Broadway* (Cambridge: Cambridge University Press, 1985) p. 266.

7. David Rabe, *Hurlyburly* (New York: Grove Press, 1985) p. 13 (Act I).

8. Christopher Durang, *Titanic*, in *Christopher Durang Explains It All for You: Six Plays* (New York: Avon Books, 1983) p. 89.

9. Statistics prepared by John Gersten, Rosenstone/Wender.

10. Bigsby, *Beyond Broadway*, p. 270.

11. Ibid., pp. 252–3.

12. Mamet, 'Chicago,' ts., 4.

Bibliography

Primary Sources

PUBLISHED PLAYS (IN CHRONOLOGICAL ORDER OF PUBLICATION)

American Buffalo (New York: Grove Press, 1977).
'Sexual Perversity in Chicago' and 'The Duck Variations' (New York: Grove Press, 1978).
'American Buffalo', 'Sexual Perversity in Chicago' and 'The Duck Variations' (London: Methuen, 1978).
A Life in the Theatre (New York: Grove Press, 1978).
The Revenge of the Space Pandas, or, Binky Rudich and the Two-Speed Clock (Chicago: Dramatic Publishing Company, 1978).
The Water Engine and Mr Happiness (New York: Grove Press, 1978).
'Reunion' and 'Dark Pony' (New York: Grove Press, 1979).
The Woods (New York: Grove Press, 1979).
The Poet and The Rent (New York: Samuel French, 1981).
Short Plays and Monologues (New York: Dramatists Play Service, 1981).
Lakeboat (New York: Grove Press, 1981).
Squirrels (New York: Samuel French, 1981).
Edmond (New York: Grove Press, 1983).
The Frog Prince (New York: Samuel French, 1983).
Glengarry Glen Ross (New York: Grove Press, 1984; London: Methuen, 1984).

Goldberg Street: Short Plays and Monologues (New York: Grove Press, 1985).
'The Shawl' and 'Prairie du Chien' (New York: Grove Press, 1985).

ESSAYS

Writing in Restaurants (New York: Penguin–Viking, 1986).

UNPUBLISHED PLAYS

Lone Canoe, or, The Explorer (typescript, 1979).
The Disappearance of the Jews (typescript, 1982). All rights retained by David Mamet.

ADAPTATIONS

Red River (adaptation of Pierre Laville's *Le Fleuve rouge*; typescript, 1982–3).
The Cherry Orchard (adaptation of Anton Chekhov's play as literally translated by Peter Nelles; typescript, 1985).

UNPUBLISHED SCREENPLAYS

The Postman Always Rings Twice (typescript, 1979).
The Verdict (typescript, 1981–2).
Things Change (with Shel Silverstein; typescript, 1984).
The Untouchables (typescript, 1985).
The House of Games (later retitled *The Tell*; typescript, 1985).

Secondary Sources

BOOKS

Bettelheim, Bruno, *The Uses Of Enchantment: The Meaning and Importance of Fairy Tales* (New York: Alfred A. Knopf, 1976).
Bigsby, C. W. E., *David Mamet*, Contemporary Writers Series (London: Methuen, 1985).
——, *A Critical Introduction to Twentieth Century American Drama*, III: *Beyond Broadway* (Cambridge: Cambridge University Press, 1985).
Campbell, Joseph, *The Hero with a Thousand Faces*, Bollingen Series, 17 (Princeton, NJ: Princeton University Press, 1949).
Cohn, Ruby, *New American Dramatists 1960–1980*, Macmillan Modern Dramatists (London: Macmillan, 1982).

Veblen, Thorstein, *The Theory Of the Leisure Class: An Economic Study of Institutions* (1899; New York: Modern Library, 1934).

ARTICLES

Allen, Jennifer, 'David Mamet's Hard Sell', *New York*, 9 April 1984, pp. 38–41.

Berbera, Jack V., 'Ethical Perversity in America: Some Observations on David Mamet's *American Buffalo*', *Modern Drama*, 24, no. 3 (1981) pp. 270–5.

Cantwell, Mary, 'David Mamet: Bulldog of the Middle Class', *Vogue*, July 1984, pp. 216–17, 281.

Christiansen, Richard, 'The Young Lion of Chicago Theatre', *Chicago Tribune Magazine*, 11 July 1982, pp. 9–19.

DeVries, Hillary, 'In David Mamet's Hands a Pen Becomes a Whip', *Christian Science Monitor*, 21 March 1984, pp. 21–2.

Ditsky, John, 'He Lets You See the Thought There: The Theatre of David Mamet', *Kansas Quarterly*, 12, no. 4 (1979) pp. 25–34.

Eder, Richard, 'David Mamet's New Realism', *New York Times Magazine*, 12 March 1978, pp. 40–3.

Freedman, Samuel G., 'The Gritty Eloquence of David Mamet', *New York Times Magazine*, 21 April 1985, pp. 32–64.

Gale, Steven H., 'David Mamet: The Plays 1972–1980', in *Essays on Contemporary American Drama*, ed. Hedwig Bock and Albert Wertheim (Munich: Max Hueber, 1981) pp. 207–23.

Gussow, Mel, 'The Daring Visions of Four New, Young Playwrights', *New York Times*, 13 February 1977, section 2, pp. 1, 9, 13.

Lawson, Steve, 'Language Equals Action', *Horizon*, November 1977, pp. 40–5.

Lewis, Patricia and Browne, Terry, 'David Mamet', in *Dictionary of Literary Biography*, VII: *Twentieth Century American Dramatists*, ed. John MacNicholas (Detroit: Gale Research Company, 1981) pp. 63–70.

Schleuter, June, and Forsyth, Elizabeth, 'America as Junkshop: The Business Ethic in David Mamet's *American Buffalo*', *Modern Drama* 26, no. 4 (1983) pp. 492–500.

Storey, Robert, 'The Making of David Mamet', *Hollins Critic*, 16, no. 4 (1979) pp. 1–11.

Terry, Clifford, 'At Work and Plays with David Mamet', *Chicago Tribune*, 8 May 1977, section 9, pp. 16–21, 26–9.

Thomas, Trevor, 'His Words Get under the Skin', *Los Angeles Times*, 17 June 1984, Calendar section, pp. 40–1.

Wetzsteon, Ross, 'David Mamet: Remember That Name', *Village Voice*, 5 July 1976, pp. 101–4.

Yakir, Don, 'The Postman's Words', *Film Comment*, March–April 1981, pp. 21–4.

ARCHIVAL COLLECTIONS

Goodman Theatre Archives, Special Collections Division, Chicago Public Library.
St Nicholas Theatre Archives. Special Collections Division, Chicago Public Library.
TOFT (Theatre on Film and Tape) Collection, Billy Rose Theatre Collection, New York Public Library at Lincoln Center.

VIDEOCASSETTES IN THE TOFT COLLECTION

The Duck Variations, scene from the production by Gerald Gutierrez, performed in *New Actors for the Classics*, 1980.
The Duck Variations, scenes from the same production performed in *Emerging Playwrights*, 1977. Includes an interview with Mamet by Richard Barr.
Edmond, directed by Gregory Mosher, Provincetown Playhouse, 1982.
A Life in the Theatre, stage version directed by Gerald Gutierrez, WNET Great Performances Series, 1979.
Reunion and *Dark Pony*, scenes from Mamet's production in 'The Playwright Directs', WNET *Camera Three*, 1979.
Reunion and *Dark Pony*, directed by Lamont Johnson, a Lion's Gate Production in association with ABS Video Enterprises, 1982.
The Water Engine, directed by Steven Schachter, New York Shakespeare Festival Production, 1978.
The Woods, directed by Ulu Grosbard, New York Public Theatre, 1979.
Sanford Meisner: The Theatre's Best Kept Secret, Playhouse Repertory, New York, 1984.

Index